God in Every Day
A Whispered Prayer

Deirdre M. Powell

ISBN 9781788125352

Designed by Messenger Publications Design Department
Typeset in Garamond Premier Pro
Printed by Hussar Books

Messenger Publications,
37 Leeson Place, Dublin D02 E5V0
www.messenger.ie

❧ CONTENTS ❧

Acknowledgements

I wish to extend my deep appreciation to a number of people for their support and assistance. Although I am the author of this book, I am well aware that I 'stand on the shoulders of giants'. First, the team at Messenger Publications were a joy to work with and had the ability to envision what this project could become. Sincere thanks to Cecilia West, Director of Messenger Publications; Kate Kiernan, Assistant Editor; Paula Nolan, Art Director Design Department; Carolanne Henry, Communications and Marketing Executive; and Fr Donal Neary SJ, Editor of *The Sacred Heart Messenger*. I wish to express my thanks to Fr Brendan McManus SJ and Jim Deeds for writing the foreword to this book.

A big thank you to my family and friends, together with all former and current colleagues. Thank you to current and former editors, writers, journalists and creative writing teachers for assistance, professionals who were instrumental in my development as a writer.

The companionship and prayerful support of lay and religious friends in the Dominican Order and in the Carmelite Order is warmly acknowledged. A special thank you to the Avila Team and participants of the 2017 Prayer School for insightful discussions. The prayerful support of friends and colleagues in the local deanery is greatly appreciated.

Finally, this book is dedicated to the memory of my dear parents, Joe and Meena Powell.

Foreword

Deirdre M. Powell's book is a great example of Ignatian spirituality in practice, helping people improve their everyday prayer life. It rightly lives up to the claim of 'Finding God in all Things'. The book reflects the incarnate God who is close and always trying to reach us through various different images of God that are present to us in everyday life. Deirdre is wonderfully creative in bringing in many dimensions of human existence. There is a strong sense of a close and intimate God who is present to us in many ways, always communicating his love to us. This is a very Ignatian idea of God active in the ordinariness of everyday life, eminently discoverable for anyone who is open and attentive.

Deirdre is a great writer, and her creative use of language tells us that she has the heart of a poet. She, herself, is inspired by God and in her writing she inspires us. Her masterful use of scripture in this book allows the reader to gain insight into the Word of God as experienced by those who wrote and read the early scriptures. She then invites us into considering the relevance of scripture in our own lives through her beautiful meditations and prayers. The invitation in this book goes even further. We are invited to search out songs, poems, pieces of art and even a secluded orchard in the heart of Dublin! Deirdre is one of life's adventurers, delighting in the hidden gems in the world around us, and she encourages us to join in the adventure. Whether in the garden, in the art gallery or around the breakfast table, this book encourages us to find God where God is.

This book will greatly aid the reader in expanding their prayer life, opening them to experience the reality of God in the ordinary details of life that have enormous meaning.

Jim Deeds & Brendan McManus SJ

Part One
Finding God in the Everyday

Introduction

The first part of this book is about finding God in everyday things. Sometimes, we can be tempted to think that God is only present in church or is only to be read about in the Bible. In fact, God can be found just as much in the pages of life. There is a saying, 'Life is a great teacher'. The spirit of this saying carries over to our relationship with God; the ordinariness of living can teach us a lot about our relationship with God.

I find great comfort in finding God in art, for example, whether it is painting, music or writing. I find that I can get lost in the beauty of the imagination but, in so doing, be drawn closer to God. Some prefer to cook or be active in the garden. These are also places where we can readily encounter God. God is just as much among the pots and pans, the seeds and sowers, as he is the brushes, instruments and artists.

God can be found in humanity and creation. These are perhaps the most important places we can encounter God in our everyday life. We are all concerned with the emerging climate crisis, and it is important to remember that God is present in creation. We must be good stewards of this earth and pass it on to the next generation. The discovery of God in humanity is perhaps the central theme of our lives and a powerful and distinctive feature of our faith.

I hope these meditations on finding God in creation, the garden, cooking, art and humanity can bring readers closer to God in everyday life. Pope Francis has encouraged us to move toward a synodal model of Church, and he has placed more emphasis than ever before on our care for creation, transforming the way faith and ecology interact. Now is the time to find God in our everyday lives, to discover the Holy Spirit at work in parts of our lives that we instinctively secularise, and to use these discoveries to enrich parish life and the life of the whole Church.

Finding God in Creation

The image of God as creator is very special. The Bible tells us that God created the heavens and the earth. He also created people in his own image, because of this people have a special relationship with God, their creator.

It's easy to imagine the creator God as very powerful. It's easy to forget that because he created everything, he can very much be found in the people and things around us. Consider a beautiful blue sky on a summer's day. The weather is warm. There are no clouds, and maybe you are relaxing on a beach. As you lie on the beach, you look upward and the vastness of the blue canvass expands before you. On closer observation, the blue sky meets the azure colour of the sea at the horizon. There is a peace and warmth to be found in such a setting. It is an everyday image created by an everyday God.

Perhaps you have a friend – maybe the friend is your husband, your wife or a good friend you met on life's journey. This person might be described as your 'anam cara'. You can relax in the presence of your soul-mate. You share the ups and downs of life together and solve the problems of the world together. There is the joy of being in the presence of your friend. The companionship that you have with this friend is a mirror of the friendship that you have with God.

Everyday God is just that. He can be found in the ordinary: the hedges in the back garden, the condensation on the window, the joyful laughter of friends and the beauty of a rustic scene. He is the creator God.

In the Beginning

Genesis 1:1
In the beginning, God created heaven and earth.

The Creation
This is the first line in the Bible, and it identifies God as creator. Here God creates heaven and earth. There have been a lot of debates about the story of Genesis! How do we make sense of the Genesis story and the discoveries of modern science? One simple but profound answer is that the Genesis story is not a scientific account; it works on a completely different level. It's important not to think of it as just a story, however. The Genesis story tells us about something that *did* happen. God *did* create all things, and God *did* create us.

Meditation
God is the creator of all things, and created the heavens and the earth. There is only one God, and God is the source of all that is. He is totally good, and all that he creates is good. The world is the creative work of one, transcendent and all-good God.

Our everyday lives are part of the work of an all-good, creator God.

Prayer
Dear God, you are our creator and the source of all that is good. We give thanks for your creation of the heavens and earth. We praise you, bless you and give thanks to you, our all-loving God.

The Second Day

Genesis 1:7–8
So God made the dome and separated the waters that were under the dome from the waters that were above the dome. And it was so. God called the dome sky. And there was evening and there was morning, the second day.

The Creation
God creates the sky and the evening and morning. The word 'dome' is used in the NRSV because the original Hebrew word suggests a gigantic metal dome. The idea here is that the dome was inserted into a single body of water in order to form a dry space from which the earth could emerge.

Meditation
It can be strange to think about the morning and evenings of our lives as creations of God. Something so absolutely ordinary, but also so unique. Every morning and evening of our lives has its own character. Could we pause in the morning and in the evening to pray? In the morning, we can look forward to the things God is going to bring to us that day. In the evening, we can reflect on all the things that did happen that day, and think about where God was present in them.

This passage of Genesis reminds me of another bible verse, Isaiah 55:9. 'For the heavens are as high above earth as my ways are above your ways, my thoughts above your thoughts.' God is our creator, but his ways and thoughts are far above ours.

Prayer
Dear God, you are our creator, but your ways are not our ways. Your ways are much higher. We ask that you bring out the best in us, little though we are. We pray to have a greater understanding of your will for us and a blending of the life that we lead here on earth with the life you have prepared for us in heaven.

Two Great Lights

Genesis 1:16
God made the two great lights – the greater light to rule the day and the lesser light to rule the night – and the stars.

The Creation
This passage refers to the creation of the sun and the moon. This part of Genesis serves as an introduction. It introduces the primordial story of human life (Genesis 2:4–11:26), the accounts of our distant ancestors (Genesis 11:27–50:26), and the whole of the Pentateuch (which comprises Genesis, Exodus, Leviticus, Numbers and Deuteronomy).

Meditation
Nowadays, it is hard to think of the sun and moon as the 'two great lights' in our lives. The artificial lights of the cities we live in, of our tablets, phones, and computer screens, are very bright in their own way. Reflecting on this passage of Genesis, we can think of the creation of these two guiding lights that accompany us during the day and night.

During the day we can feel the warmth of the sun and be reminded of the goodness and mercy of Christ – the light of the world. His goodness and mercy shine on us like sunshine. At night, we can look up at the majesty of the night sky and see the beauty of the moon and stars, giving thanks for the expansiveness of creation.

In *Laudato Si'* Pope Francis has urged us to take care of our common home, which is threatened by climate change. Let's reflect on the world God has created and our role in taking care of it.

Prayer
Dear God, we give thanks for the splendour of your creation: from the wonder of tiny atoms and molecules, which we cannot see, to the vast expanse of the heavens, space and beyond. We give thanks for what we can see in the world and the heavens, and we look to the future with hope that we may be able to explore what lies beyond our current knowledge.

Every Kind

Genesis 1:21
So God created the great sea monsters and every living creature that moves, of every kind, with which the waters swarm, and every winged bird of every kind. And God saw that it was good.

The Creation
God creates life in the oceans and in the air.

Meditation
This passage of Genesis really evokes the vastness of the oceans and the diversity of life found there, from the tiny, seemingly insignificant plankton right up to huge basking sharks and whales. We are reminded that God created creatures of 'every kind', and that all of what he created was good. Can we take time to reflect on the diversity of God's creation? What can we learn about ourselves and our world, knowing that God made it so diverse?

Prayer
We give thanks to you God for the beauty of creation, for the birds of the air and the creatures of the sea. We say thank you for the companionship of these animals and are grateful for the fact that they are often a source of food for us. Almighty and ever-living God, we praise you for your generosity toward us.

Wild Animals

Genesis 1:25

God made the wild animals of the earth of every kind, and the cattle of every kind, and everything that creeps upon the ground of every kind. And God saw that it was good.

The Creation

God creates all the animals that walk (or creep!) on the earth.

Meditation

A farmer once told me that cows today are nowhere near as friendly as they once were! I wondered what he could possibly mean. In his youth farmers worked closely with their cattle. Over time, everything became more mechanised and automatic. The cattle no longer had that close relationship with the farmer. They had become estranged, if you can believe it.

We often miss the beauty of creation in the form of the animals we share our lives with. Dogs serve as protectors, companions, even guides to the blind and deaf. We should give thanks for all the animals God has created.

Prayer

Dear Lord, we give thanks for all animals, both wild and domestic, and all the creatures that creep along the earth also. We thank you for their creation. May we always be kind to animals in our care, whether they are companion animals or working creatures. We give glory to you, creator God, and we ask you to watch over the animals, as well as over humankind.

In His Image

Genesis 1:27
So God created humankind in his image, in the image of God he created them; male and female he created them.

The Creation
A big moment for us! God creates human beings, including the first man and woman, Adam and Eve.

Meditation
This passage of Genesis tells us something important. We are created in the image of God. Each of us is precious and is a temple of the Holy Spirit. We need to recognise how precious each person is: our parents, spouses, brothers, sisters, children, extended family, friends, neighbours, even strangers.

We can ask God for the gift of understanding other people. We can ask especially for the ability to empathise with those who are different from us. Just like God created 'every kind' of creature in the sea, he created every one of us.

This passage of Genesis reminds me of a famous passage of Matthew's Gospel. 'Truly I tell you, just as you did it to one of the least of these who are members of my family, you did it to me' (Matthew 25:40). One place we can be guaranteed to encounter God in our daily lives is in the people around us.

Prayer
We give thanks to you, creator God for making us in your own image. Often, we forget how precious we are to you. We are all equal in your sight. Help us to be aware of and be grateful for the gift of life that you have given us.

Seventh Day

Genesis 2:2–3
And on the seventh day God finished the work that he had done, and he rested on the seventh day from all the work that he had done. So God blessed the seventh day and hallowed it, because on it God rested from all the work that he had done in creation.

The Creation
God is finished working, and he rests. The mention of the seventh day in Genesis 2:2 is the climax of the whole account, and it is repeated in Genesis 2:3. God is the focus. The practice of keeping the Sabbath holy is not, in fact, instituted by this passage, but it lays the foundation for subsequent practice. It is worth mentioning that Sabbath observance was linked with creation, and that it was also linked with Exodus.

Meditation
God worked for six days, but he rested on the seventh. It's easy to think of rest in a negative way, as *doing nothing*. We can ask God to bless our work but also our free time. We can enjoy leisure and be grateful to God for it. Let's spend our Sundays going to Mass and enjoying free time with family and friends.

Prayer
As you, creator God, kept holy the Sabbath day, we ask for the grace to do the same. We ask that you bless our work and our leisure time. It is good to take a break in life – may we recognise the value of our free time.

The Word

John 1:1–3

In the beginning was the Word, and the Word was with God, and the Word was God. He was in the beginning with God. All things came into being through him, and without him not one thing came into being.

The Creation

John begins his Gospel with a description of the Word of God (John 1:1–3). John describes Jesus as the creative, life-giving and light-giving Word of God that has come to earth in human form (John 1:1–18). Truly, Jesus is the Son of God who, while remaining God and Lord, became a man and our brother. From the beginning of God's creation, his purpose for us is that we would be fully united with him.

Meditation

This passage from John's Gospel brings us back to the beginning of everything. While the passages from Genesis we have read describe in detail all the many kinds of thing God has created – the earth, sky, sun, moon, stars, animals and people – this passage from John is powerfully inclusive. Not one thing came into being without God. We can see that God has made a permanent dwelling in our world, and that he has had a purpose for us from the very beginning.

Can we think of our everyday lives as part of this 'big picture' that stretches back to the creation of everything? What would it change about our everyday lives if we thought of them as part of God's creation?

Prayer

Dear God, we give thanks for your creation and for the gift of Jesus, your Son, made man. We ask for the grace to fully appreciate his presence among us and to aspire to full unity with you.

Reflection:
Recognition

'He was in the world, and the world came into being through him; yet the world did not know him' (John 1:10).

How often have we failed to recognise Jesus in others? How often have we conveniently overlooked Jesus in the poor, for example? It is so easy to turn away from those in need.

In this passage from John it is the world, and not just any one of us, who 'did not know him'. The world did not recognise the Word, even though it 'came into being through him'. In life we often fail to recognise Jesus in others, just as others often fail to recognise him in us. Sometimes being a parent, for example, is a thankless job. Sometimes we must do the difficult work of caring for someone who can not care for themselves, or even is no longer able to recognise us. These are not easy situations for either the carer or the cared for. What we must remember, however, is that Jesus is present in both.

With Genesis as our guide, we've seen how God is present in creation – in the basic stuff of our everyday lives, our mornings, evenings and nights. We can also reflect on how the 'world did not know him'. As much as God is present in creation, it's not always going to be easy to find him. If we feel that we can't, it is not necessarily 'our fault'. We can remember that 'the world did not know him'.

Peter and John were imprisoned for teaching that Jesus had risen from the dead. When they were released from prison, they went back to the community and told people what had happened.

'When they heard it they lifted up their voice to God with one heart. "Master," they prayed, "it is you who made the sky and earth and sea, and everything in them"' (Acts 4:24).

In that time of difficulty Peter and John and their Christian community prayed. An enhanced prayer life can help us to recognise God in creation and especially in the people around us, including the poor.

In prayer we can recognise God as the creator of sky, earth, sea and everything in them, and in prayer we can bring this recognition into our daily lives.

Prayer

We pray for the grace to recognise you, Jesus, in the presence of others. We give thanks for all those people who are the unsung heroes in our lives. We praise you, creator God, for you made the sky and earth and sea, and everything in them.

Finding God in the Garden

O ne of my favourite gardens is an orchard in the suburbs of Dublin. There is a small summer house to relax in and enjoy the delights of the garden: the trees with their bending arms, the neatly cut grass and the sweet singing of the birds. The orchard is secluded. It is a haven of peace and sometimes feels like a piece of heaven. The orchard has an 'Olde Worlde' feeling about it. I can imagine running into a character from a Jane Austen novel there.

In the Bible there are several times when God or Jesus is referred to as being present in a garden. In the Old Testament, God was present in the Garden of Eden, where he walked with Adam and Eve. In the New Testament, Jesus suffered in the Garden of Gethsemane before his passion and death. After the resurrection, he was also mistaken for the gardener by Mary of Magdalene.

The garden is a great place to find God in an everyday way. It is strange to think of God as being interested in sowing flowers and vegetables, digging for worms, or just being close to the earth that is often the source of new life. Yet, God is a gardener! Sometimes he is the great 'sower' and at other times he is the great 'mower'. God tends to his garden, and we can find him in ours.

Lilies of the Field

Matthew 6:28–29

'And why are you anxious about clothing? Consider the lilies of the field, how they grow: they neither toil nor spin, yet I tell you, even Solomon in all his glory was not arrayed like one of these.'

In the Garden

In this passage from Matthew's Gospel, Jesus tells us about the beautiful lilies of the field; the lilies fulfil their purpose in beauty, yet they do not toil in the fields. It is as though they grow without effort. In all his glory, King Solomon was not comparable with the lilies in the field. Saints are often portrayed in the presence of lilies: in medieval paintings of the Annunciation, the Archangel Gabriel extends a lily toward the Blessed Mother. This lily symbolises her purity, innocence and goodness. Following the symbolism, artists often portray virginal saints with white lilies.[1]

Meditation

The avid gardener might disagree with Jesus! Caring for flowers in the garden can be a lot of work. But Jesus is right, no amount of human labour can create something as beautiful and fulfilled as a flower. If we pay attention to the flowers, we can find not only a glory greater than Solomon's but also an important lesson on anxiety.

In this passage, Jesus is encouraging us not to be anxious. later in this same passage, he assures us that Our Heavenly Father will provide. We can ask for the gift to accept each day as it comes. We can ask for the grace to trust in God. Like the flower, we can understand that God has created us and will provide.[2]

Prayer

Dear Lord, we thank you for supporting us in our daily lives. We ask forgiveness for the times when we have ignored your goodness. We pray for those who are in need and ask for the grace and opportunity to help them.

1   Madeline Pecora Nugent, 'Lily of Purity', Messenger of St Anthony (website), 30 April 2015, https://www.messengersaintanthony.com/content/lily-purity.
2   This meditation was partly inspired by Jack Wellman, 'Lilies of the Field', Patheos (website), www.patheos.com/blogs/christiancrier/2015/11/16/lilies-of-the-field-bible-verse-meaning-and-study.

In the Wilderness

Isaiah 41:19
I will put in the wilderness the cedar,
  the acacia, the myrtle, and the olive;
I will set in the desert the cypress,
  the plane and the pine together,

In the Garden
This passage provides a picture of the Paradise of God, completing a vision of the future from elsewhere in Isaiah (51:3). There are two groups of four and three trees, which may constitute the symbolic seven and so may have a mystical significance.[3] The important detail is that God will bring a great abundance to the wilderness. This abundance is also marked by diversity: the trees mentioned in this passage are found at this time across Lebanon, Palestine and Egypt.

Meditation
God will bring abundance to the wilderness. He will provide for his people. He is the planter and gardener not just of trees, but also of our souls. We can see that God's closeness to us in the garden is an expression of his care for us. The richness of nature is connected to the richness of our spiritual lives, and we have a duty of care – as Pope Francis has emphasised in *Laudato Si'* – toward our common home.

Even where things seem desperate or impossible, God has the power to bring life in abundance. This promise is echoed in John 10:10, 'I came that they may have life, and have it abundantly.'

Prayer
Dear Lord, you console us in times of need and in times of abundance. So often, you provide for our needs, and we are sometimes unaware of it. We give thanks for your presence in our world.

---

3   *Eliott's Commentary for English Readers*, 'Isaiah 41', StudyLight (website), https://www.studylight.org/commentaries/eng/ebc/isaiah-41.html.

The Mustard Seed

Luke 13:9
It [the kingdom of God] is like a mustard seed, which a man took and planted in his garden. It grew and became a tree, and the birds perched in its branches.

In the Garden
The mustard plant would have been a common sight for the people of Jesus' time. The analogy Jesus draws in this passage would have been familiar to them as well. From a minute grain it grows as high as a fruit tree. Jesus is telling us here that the kingdom of God starts small but grows into something life-giving and big.

Meditation
Jesus tells us that something small, like a mustard seed, can turn out to have a great influence. The kingdom of God comes into being in a humble way. Jesus works quietly and invisibly in our lives. We're not always aware of him! We can take the time to breathe in and out, becoming more aware of God's presence in our lives. The seeds of the garden remind us that the kingdom of God grows from small things, simple acts of kindness and service.

Prayer
Dear Lord, I pray that the kingdom of God will grow in my heart through simple acts of kindness that I offer to family, friends and strangers in my life.

Time of Singing

Song of Solomon 2:12

The flowers appear on the earth, the time of singing has come, and the voice of the turtledove is heard in our land.

In the Garden

Matthew Poole notes that this passage is associated with the coming of spring.[4] There is a mystical significance to spring here. It is associated with salvation and grace. The appearance of the flowers marks a change from 2:11 'winter is past, the rain is over and gone'. We can all think of a time when we've looked out the window, only to notice that winter has finally passed.

Meditation

Spring is a time when we anticipate growth and new life. It can remind us of God's grace as well the comforts of the Holy Spirit. Even when times are difficult, we can know that the winter will pass and the rain will be over and gone. God will make 'flowers appear on the earth'. We can reflect on God's love for each of us and look forward to the surprises and discoveries his grace will bring into our lives.

Prayer

Dear Lord, we thank you for your goodness to us in springtime, with the emergence of new flowers, new leaves on the trees and new life that is expressed in creatures around us. We ask for the grace to recognise this beauty and to recognise your care for us.

---

4   Matthew Poole, 'Poole's English Annotations of the Bible', StudyLight (website), https://www.studylight. org/commentaries/eng/mpc/song-of-solomon-2.html#verse-1.

The Garden of Eden

Genesis 2:8
And the Lord planted a Garden in Eden, in the east, and there he put the man whom he had formed.

In the Garden
In an earlier chapter we encountered God the creator. We looked in detail at the story of Genesis. God is also portrayed as a gardener in Genesis. Genesis 2:9 says, 'Out of the ground the Lord God made grow every tree that was delightful to look at and good for food, with the tree of life in the middle of the garden, and the tree of the knowledge of good and evil.' It's important to understand that God did not create the Garden of Eden as a paradise for human beings, but as his garden.

Meditation
God planted a Garden in Eden that was full of beautiful trees and food that was good to eat. The food on our tables comes from God too. In a more automated and globalised world, we forget or never even learn where our food comes from! These days the things we buy in the supermarket come from the gardens of the whole world. We can be grateful for this food, and we can remember those who don't have as much as we do. With Pope Francis we can work to protect the environment and ensure that everyone – locally and globally – has enough to eat.

Prayer
Bountiful Jesus, we give thanks to you for providing us with our daily bread. We ask you to help us to care for our earthly home and to secure our environment.

The Garden of Gethsemane

John 18:1

After Jesus had spoken these words, he went out with his disciples across the Kidron valley, where there was a garden, which he and his disciples entered.

In the Garden

The Garden of Gethsemane was the place where Jesus went with his disciples to pray the night prior to his crucifixion. It was familiar to the disciples because it was close to the natural route that leads from the Temple to the summit of the Mount of Olives and the ridge leading to Bethany. Today, there are eight olive trees in the Garden of Gethsemane. Research reported in 2012 revealed that three of the eight ancient trees dated from the middle of the twelfth century and that all eight originated as cuttings from a single parent tree. It is possible that the present-day Gethsemane olives are descendants of one tree that was in the garden during the time of Christ.

Meditation

The garden isn't just a place where we can find a sense of renewal or new beginnings. It can also be a place of protection, shelter and even tradition. Like the olive trees in the Garden of Gethsemane, we are connected to a religious tradition that goes back many centuries, originating from the parent tree of Jesus. In the garden, we can be reminded of God's protection and his presence throughout human history.

Prayer

Dear Lord, we are tempted so often in life to be self-sufficient. We pray for the gift of recognising our dependency on and need for you.

Rushes, Reeds and Rivers

Exodus 2:3

When she could hide him no longer she got a papyrus basket for him, and plastered it with bitumen and pitch; she put the child in it and placed it among the reeds on the bank of the river.

In the Garden

Exodus 2:1–10 describes the birth and early life of Moses. His mother hides her son, thereby defying Pharaoh's order. Once Moses becomes too old to conceal, she places him in a basket on the Nile, in a deliberate attempt to have him adopted. Pharaoh's daughter finds the baby and in the end, she hires Moses' own mother to be his wet nurse. In Exodus 2:3, we witness the importance of nature, as the basket is made from rushes and is placed among the reeds of the River Nile.

Meditation

By giving away her son, Moses' mother ensured that he lived – an incredible example of the love of mothers. The river and the reeds that grew on its banks helped Moses and his mother. They concealed and carried Moses to safety. We can be confronted with difficult choices in life, just like Moses' mother. When we have to make hard decisions, we can lean on those around us, and depend on their strength.

Maybe a walk by the river could help us to remember the resources that are all around us, hidden in plain sight. Following the journey of the river, we can think of Moses' journey, our own journey in life, and the people, especially parents and guardians, who have supported us along the way.

Prayer

We give thanks to you, Lord, for our parents and guardians, together with teachers and all those who nurture and educate young people.

Vineyards, Gardens and Fruit

Amos 9:14

I will restore the fortunes of my people Israel,
     and they shall rebuild the ruined cities and inhabit them;
they shall plant vineyards and drink their wine,
     and they shall make gardens and eat their fruit.

In the Garden

Amos 9:14 is part of a wider passage Amos 9:11–15 that probably constitutes an editorial supplement to the Book of Amos, added to bring the book into harmony with the positive thrust of the prophetic books in general, particularly those written following the Exile, when the final edition of Amos was most likely completed.[5] This passage emphasises that destruction was not God's last word for Israel – despite their suffering, they will have gardens again.

Meditation

This passage is an injection of hope for the people of Israel. We can see that nature and the bounty of nature play an important role in that hope. Not only will the cities be rebuilt, but vineyards and gardens will be planted, bringing wine and fruit for the people of Israel. Hope and celebration are important to us as Christians. The vineyards and fruit trees of the earth can remind us of the need for hope and celebration. We can think of John 2:1–11, where at a wedding Jesus turns water to wine. As Christians, we can hope for a better future.

Prayer

Dear Lord, we pray for the presence of hope in our lives: hope for a better future, hope for good health and hope for those who are in need of peace and justice. We give you thanks for all the good things you give us from the earth, including fruit from the fruit trees and wine from the vineyards.

---

5   *New American Bible* (revised ed.), Amos 9:11–15 (commentary), United States Conference of Catholic Bishops, https://bible.usccb.org/bible/amos/9.

The Rose of Sharon

Song of Songs: 2:1–2

I am a rose of Sharon,
    a lily of the valleys.
As a lily among brambles,
    so is my love among maidens.

In the Garden

In this extract, Our Lord is referred to as the 'rose of Sharon', an exquisite flower. He is almighty, all-loving, all-powerful and all-holy. It is worth noting that Sharon constitutes a rich region of land that lies between Mount Carmel and Jaffa in the Mediterranean coast; some of the richest soil in the world may be found there. The region is enhanced by beautiful flowers, mainly roses, and these roses are greatly prized in this Eastern area because they are used in rose water. The flowers in our own gardens can remind us of the all-loving presence of Jesus.

Meditation

We meditate on the beauty of roses, as well as of lilies. The rose is a symbol of love, and Christ is the 'rose of Sharon', who loves us dearly. When we are given a rose or bouquet of roses, we recognise it is a beautiful gift that symbolises the affection of the gift-giver for us. There is a great feeling when we receive this flower with its lovely bloom and fragrant scent. Jesus, you are also like this – you are love and joy at its best.

Prayer

Dear Lord, we give thanks for the gifts of love and joy in our hearts. We give thanks also for the times when we recognise these gifts from you, and we especially remember those who feel alone or unloved in the world. We pray that the peace and joy of Christ will be with them.

Finding God in Art

One of the most beautiful ways of getting to know God is through art. Imagine God as a painter, musician, writer or poet! Years ago, I used to work in a publishing firm, and I used to imagine God as the great 'Editor in the Sky' who was carefully watching over every missing comma and grammatical mistake, but who was trying to guide me in the right (*write*) direction.

Spend some time in an art gallery and admire the beauty of the paintings. The four paintings mentioned in this chapter are by Murillo, Rembrandt, Eeckhout and Caravaggio and are available to view in the National Gallery of Ireland in Dublin. The subjects are Christian in nature, and they reflect the beauty of Christ.

Try to imagine God as a musician. I remember a famous scientist once describing that he felt very close to God whenever he heard a symphony. Music can evoke strong emotions in the listener, and our hearts can be touched by the sweetness and simplicity of a song or the majesty of a symphony. The four pieces mentioned in this chapter are well known: 'How Great Thou Art', 'Ave Verum Corpus', 'The Hallelujah Chorus' and 'Gabriel's Oboe'. They can often be heard in a Christian context.

Finally, think of God as a writer or poet. God is often a source of inspiration for the writer, and if we take the time we can find God in poetry and in prose. I have always felt that 'Pied Beauty' and 'A Christmas Childhood' were two of the most beautifully reflective poems that a person could read – 'Glory be to God for dappled things.'

The Holy Family

Luke 2:7

'And she gave birth to her firstborn son and wrapped him in bands of cloth ... '

The Painting

The painting *The Holy Family* by Bartolomé Esteban Murillo (1617–1682) was painted in the late 1640s as an oil on canvas. This particular work depicts the Holy Family in everyday life as a humble family, with Joseph's carpentry tools visible in the background. Joseph is portrayed as the caring father who is about to hand over his son to the Virgin Mary; Our Lady reaches out to the young child.

Go see the painting at the National Gallery of Ireland or go online at: http://onlinecollection.nationalgallery.ie/objects/3177/the-holy-family.

Meditation

The simplicity of this family scene is striking. There is a palpable warmth and intimacy about the picture, which depicts nothing more than Joseph holding his son, Jesus, in the company of Mary.

The simplicity of the scene brings to mind the ordinary, everyday nature of family life. Parents work hard to provide for their children. The rush of today's world – getting a son or daughter to hockey practice or football practice, to birthday parties where teeth are sugar-tested and to dentist appointments where teeth are put right – was alien to Mary and Joseph's time. The joy of love between parents and their children, so clearly depicted in *The Holy Family*, however, unites us.

Let's take the time to notice God's presence in the everyday nature of family life. Families aren't always easy, but in them we can find a powerful expression of the joy of love.

Prayer

Let us pray: we give thanks to the Lord for family life and for the experience of the joy of love. We pray for the grace to recognise that love is always patient and kind, never envious or boastful.

The Flight into Egypt

Matthew 2:13

'Now after they had left, an angel of the Lord appeared to Joseph in a dream and said, "Get up, take the child and his mother, and flee to Egypt, and remain there until I tell you; for Herod is about to search for the child, to destroy him."'

The Painting

Landscape with the Rest on the Flight into Egypt was painted by Rembrandt van Rijn (1606–1669) in 1647 and was painted as an oil on wood panel. Although the subject of the flight into Egypt appears to occupy a small place in this painting, our attention is drawn to the fire, which is one of the sources of light in the picture. Rembrandt chose to emphasise the nocturnal hilly landscape, which is illuminated by many sources of light.

Go see the painting at the National Gallery of Ireland or go online at: http://www.nationalgallery.ie/art-and-artists/highlights-collection/landscape-rest-flight-egypt-rembrandt-van-rijn-1606-1669.

Meditation

There are two striking features about this painting. The presence of the light of the campfire reminds us of the notion that Jesus is 'the light of the world', but there is also sorrow. To place the journey in context, the Holy Family are travelling to Egypt in order to escape Herod, who seeks to kill Jesus. This must have been a terrifying experience. Yet, the Holy Family overcome these difficulties and arrive safely as emigrants in Egypt. Rembrandt's painting reminds us that life is not all 'plain-sailing'. There is darkness as well as light in every life. Rembrandt captures in a startling way just how small the Holy Family must have felt on their journey to Egypt. When we feel small, let's keep in mind that everyone feels this way sometimes. Let's remember that, just as it was for the Holy Family, God is with us on our journey.

Prayer

Dear Lord, we ask for the strength to overcome difficulties in life. We pray also for migrant communities across the world.

Christ in the Synagogue at Nazareth

Luke 4:15
'He began to teach in their synagogues and was praised by everyone.'

The Painting
When Jesus began his Galilean ministry, he preached in many of the synagogues in Galilee, including the synagogue at Nazareth. Luke's Gospel says that he was handed the Book of Isaiah and recited from it. When he finished, he returned the scripture and spoke to those present, saying, 'This text is being fulfilled today even while you are listening.' The painting *Christ in the Synagogue at Nazareth* was painted in 1658 by the Dutch artist Gerbrand van den Eeckhout (1621–1674).

Go see the painting at the National Gallery of Ireland or go online at: http://onlinecollection.nationalgallery.ie/objects/6527/christ-in-the-synagogue-at-nazareth.

Meditation
In this painting we immediately note the kindly, patient face of Christ, gesturing as he teaches the other scholars at the synagogue. Attention is drawn to the figure of Christ. He is bathed in light while many of the remaining figures are in the shadows. Christ's listeners are intent on each word that he speaks.

Here, we see Christ in the role of teacher and preacher. We can reflect on the many good and gifted teachers we have had over the years. The role of the teacher holds a special place in everyday life (see page 102). The place of the preacher in daily life is also noteworthy. We can all give thanks for the many thought-provoking sermons we have heard from dedicated preachers of the Gospel.

Prayer
We give thanks, Lord, for the role of teachers and preachers in our lives. We ask you to bless and protect them and to bless their listeners too.

The Taking of Christ

Luke 22:47

'While he was still speaking, suddenly a crowd came, and the one called Judas, one of the twelve, was leading them. He approached Jesus to kiss him; 48 but Jesus said to him, "Judas, is it with a kiss that you are betraying the Son of Man?"'

The Painting

The disciple Judas had agreed to betray Jesus for thirty pieces of silver and to hand him over to the chief priests, guards and elders. By kissing Jesus, Judas identified him to the crowd. The painting *The Taking of Christ* by Michelangelo Merisi da Caravaggio (1571–1610) was painted as an oil on canvas in 1602. The focus of the painting is on the action of Judas and the Temple guards on an unresisting Jesus. A fleeing St John the Evangelist is also portrayed.

Go see the painting at the National Gallery of Ireland or go online at: https://www.nationalgallery.ie/art-and-artists/highlights-collection/taking-christ-michelangelo-merisi-da-caravaggio.

Meditation

In this painting, the look of pain on Christ's face is noteworthy – he is aware of what lies ahead in terms of his passion. Think of the sorrow he must feel as a result of being betrayed by his disciple, Judas. No doubt we can all identify times in our lives when we have felt betrayed by people we thought we knew well, maybe by a friend or even a family member.

The incarnation has brought God and humanity into an intimate relationship. Let's reflect on God's intimate understanding of our pain. In Caravaggio's painting we can see that God has a first-hand knowledge of betrayal and suffering.

Prayer

For the times we feel we have been betrayed, Lord, we ask for the grace to overcome this sorrow. We also ask for the grace to forgive those who have hurt us.

'How Great Thou Art'

'Then sings my soul, My Saviour God to Thee, How great thou art! How great thou art … '

The Music

This beautiful Christian hymn, 'How Great Thou Art' is based on a Swedish traditional melody and a poem written by the pastor Carl Boberg (1859–1940) in Mönsterås, Sweden, in 1885. The inspiration for the poem arose as Boberg was walking home from church near the Swedish town of Kronobäck and listening to church bells. Boberg's attention was drawn by a sudden storm, and then just as suddenly as the storm had appeared, it subsided. The transition from sudden storm to peaceful calm observed by Boberg over Mönsterås Bay inspired the writing of the hymn.[6]

Meditation

This hymn is a beautiful reflection of God as artist and musician. The refrain (cited above) notes how our souls give glory to God by singing 'How great thou art.' This hymn reminds me of an experience I had walking along a tree-lined trail located beside a blue bay in County Donegal. The sun was shining, the birds were singing and the experience was one of complete peace. This tranquil experience of nature reminds me of how great God is. As a piece of music, this hymn has often been sung at the close of Mass in my local parish church – a lovely hymn in a local setting highlighting the notion of 'everyday God'.

We can reflect on how God is both great and accessible. Like Boberg we can be taken aback by how God's greatness lies just outside the door of our home or church. God's greatness is great *and* right at hand.

Prayer

We give glory to God in the highest as our souls sing sweetly, 'How great thou art.'

6   For more information on Boberg, see Jon Little, 'Behind the Song: Carl Boberg, "How Great Thou Art"', American Songwriter (website), https://americansongwriter.com/behind-the-song-carl-boberg-how-great-thou-art.

Ave Verum Corpus K.618.

Ave verum corpus, Natum de Maria virgine; Vere passum immolatum In crucis pro homine. Cuius latus perforatum Unda fluxit et sanguine. Esto nobis praegustatum In mortis examine.

Hail, true body, Born of the virgin Mary; who has truly suffered, slaughtered on the cross for humanity. Whose side was pierced, pouring out water and blood. Be a foretaste for us during our ordeal of death.

The Music

The beautiful forty-six-bar motet in D major, with its gentle, undulating melodic line, is a setting of the Latin hymn 'Ave verum corpus'. Mozart composed the piece for the feast of Corpus Christi and the work is scored for SATB choir, string instruments and organ. Mozart wrote the motet for his friend Anton Stoll, who was the church musician of St Stephan in the town of Baden bei Wien, Austria.[7]

Meditation

This beautiful hymn is Eucharistic in nature and calls to mind the sacrifice of Christ on the cross for humanity. It is often sung in my local church at communion.

The piece reminds us of the everyday sacrifices that each of us is called to make in our lives. A mother may take on an extra job, so that she can pay her daughter's school fees. A son may give up a part of his free time to act as a primary carer for his elderly mother. Each day, we are called to make sacrifices, so that we will grow in holiness.

Prayer

Dear Lord, give me the wisdom and understanding to sacrifice in order to grow in holiness today.

7   Background on this piece of music taken from, Betsy Schwarm, 'Mozart, W.A.: Ave Verum Corpus, K 618', Britannica website, https://www.britannica.com/topic/Ave-Verum-Corpus-K-618.

The Hallelujah Chorus

Hallelujah (x5); For the Lord God Omnipotent reigneth; Hallelujah (x4); The kingdom of this world; is become the kingdom of our Lord; And of His Christ (x2); And He shall reign for ever and ever; forever and ever (x2) ...

The Music
The famous Hallelujah chorus from the English-language oratorio 'Messiah' by Georg Frideric Handel (1685–1759) is possibly one of the most uplifting and recognisable choruses in musical history. The scriptural text was compiled by Charles Jennens from the King James Bible and from the Coverdale Psalter. The work is distinguished from most of Handel's other oratorios by an orchestral restraint, a quality that was not adopted by Mozart and other later arrangers of the music. 'Messiah' was first performed in Dublin in Fishamble Street on 13 April 1742, and received its London premiere almost a year later.

Meditation
Many years ago, I attended a performance of 'The Hallelujah Chorus' in our local church and felt transformed by the experience. It was a Christmas-time performance and the audience, musicians and singers were in a festive spirit. It was a beautiful evening of music and a great way to express praise of God at the same time.

The words of this chorus express praise and say that the kingdom of this world is to become the kingdom of Our Lord. The music helps us to praise and worship God in song, which we frequently do at Mass. The words help us to remember that God is all around us, even in this world.

Prayer
Let us 'give glory to God in the highest and peace to his people on earth.'

'Gabriel's Oboe'

'Praise him with fanfare of trumpet, praise him with harp and lyre ... Let everything that breathes praise Yahweh.' (Psalm 150)

The Music

The oboe is a type of double reed woodwind instrument that is usually made of wood, but it may also be fabricated from synthetic materials, such as resin, plastic or hybrid composites. 'Gabriel's Oboe' is the main theme from the 1986 film *The Mission* and was composed by Italian composer Ennio Morricone. The theme features prominently in the film when the protagonist, Jesuit Father Gabriel, walks up to a waterfall and begins to play his oboe, with the aim of befriending the Guarani natives with his music, so that he can undertake his missionary work in the New World.

Meditation

This beautiful work with its undulating melodic line brings great peace to my soul. It is something of a church favourite, and I have often played it (on the organ) at Mass, weddings and funerals, with its warm, melodic line, where the notes soar and are uplifting. The music is as though it could be played by angels, and although the 'Gabriel' in the title of the piece refers to the film's protagonist, sometimes I think of the Angel Gabriel as a potential musician. This is a beautiful work that brings joy to my heart.

Reflect on the unexpected ways that music can connect us to God. Often, music acts as God's messenger – visiting us out of the blue, just as Gabriel visited Mary. Can we hear God speaking to us through music?

Prayer

'Give me joy in my heart, keep me praising. Give me joy in my heart I pray; give me joy in my heart, keep me praising, keep me praising till the end of the day.' (Traditional hymn, author unknown).

'Pied Beauty'

Glory be to God for dappled things –
  For skies of couple-colour as a brinded cow;
    For rose-moles all in stipple upon trout that swim;
Fresh-firecoal chestnut falls; finches wings;
  Landscape plotted and pieced – fold, fallow, and plough;
    And all trades, their gear and tackle and trim.[8]

The Poem

This poem by Gerard Manley Hopkins SJ (1844–1889) celebrates the work of God and invites the reader to do the same. The word 'pied' means having two or more colours; it is this quality of variety that the poet most admires about the work of God. The piece is a type of hymn of praise to God that sees God's majesty both in nature's sheer variety as well as in people's labours and in the abstract categories that people use to understand their experience of the world.

Meditation

Let us meditate on the beauty of God's creation – the glory of 'dappled things', farm animals and fish. In spring and especially in summer, we are aware of the sweetness of bird song. The joy of the dawn chorus and the evening chorus is very beautiful. We give thanks to God for the beauty of roses, of tulips, of primroses and all wildflowers. We praise God for the gift of his creation in the form of each other; we are each unique.

  Hopkins' poem can make us think about the diversity and uniqueness of the natural world. Pope Francis calls us to care for our common home (*Laudato Si'*) and to care for one another through social friendship (*Fratelli Tutti*) – let's take time to appreciate and show care for our own uniqueness and the uniqueness of the world we live in.

Prayer

We give thanks to you, Almighty God, for the beauty of your creation, the earth and all that is in it, including the beauty of humankind. May we be grateful for the gift of each other.

8   Gerard Manley Hopkins, 'Pied Beauty', Poetry Foundation, https://www.poetryfoundation.org/poems/44399/pied-beauty.

'A Christmas Childhood'

Outside in the cow-house my mother
Made the music of milking;
The light of her stable-lamp was a star
And the frost of Bethlehem made it twinkle.[9]

The Poem

This extract is from a poem entitled 'A Christmas Childhood' by Patrick Kavanagh (1904–1967) and was written during 1940–1943. This is a memory poem in which the poet describes a magical and mysterious time from childhood, namely, Christmas when he was six years of age. In this poem, the ordinary becomes extraordinary. According to Kavanagh, 'adulthood blinds us to the beauty, freshness and innocence of childhood, but it can be recaptured occasionally, especially at Christmas time.'[10]

Meditation

Let us reflect on the simplicity and beauty of the Christ-child at Christmas. Here was God, made man, and he came amongst us as a child in a manger, in the presence of his parents, shepherds, wise men and farm animals. It was a simple, humble and beautiful birthday. We give thanks, O Lord, for your goodness to us at Christmas time and throughout the year.

Prayer

Dear Jesus, you come to us in simplicity at Christmas time. Help us to recapture the wonder and amazement of this festive season and to remember its beauty throughout the year. We give you thanks, dear Jesus.

9   Patrick Kavanagh, 'A Christmas Childhood', A Poem for Ireland (website), https://apoemforireland.rte.ie/shortlist/a-christmas-childhood/.
10 'A Poem for Ireland: A Christmas Childhood', RTÉ (website), https://apoemforireland.rte.ie/shortlist/a-christmas-childhood.

Finding God in Food

Sometimes, I like to think of God as a cook! In the New Testament, Jesus cooks breakfast for his disciples on the shores of the Sea of Tiberias (John 21:1–17). This is the only recorded example of Jesus actually cooking in the Bible. It is a beautiful, touching image because it is so homely, ordinary and everyday. I love to cook, and I like to imagine that God is present in my kitchen as I cook among the pots and pans. It reminds me of the saying of St Teresa of Ávila, that 'God walks among the pots and pans.'

Jesus shared plenty of meals with his disciples and friends. Food plays an important role in the New Testament. At the Wedding Feast of Cana (John 2:1–11) Jesus turned water into wine so that a young couple would not be embarrassed. This scene is Eucharistic in tradition. It pre-figures the Last Supper, where Jesus turns bread and wine into his precious body and blood.

Even in today's media, the importance of cooking is recognised in a Catholic context – TV chef Fr Leo Patalinghug from EWTN talks about food and faith with Catholics, as he cooks delicious meals and offers Church teachings in bite-sized portions.

Perhaps it is fitting to conclude this introduction with a prayer of grace before meals: 'Bless us, O Lord, and these thy gifts, which of thy bounty we are about to receive through Christ Our Lord, Amen.'

If you find that too much of a mouthful, some American friends of mine used to use a simpler prayer: 'God is good, God is great, thank you God for what is on my plate!'

Breakfast with Jesus

John 21:9–14
When they had gone ashore, they saw a charcoal fire there, with fish on it, and bread.

The Meal
This is a post-resurrection story that takes place on the shores of the Sea of Tiberias. Jesus cooks breakfast for the disciples when they return from fishing. They are hungry after their night's work, and Jesus gives his disciples fish and bread. The setting provides the backdrop to the famous incident where Jesus asks Peter three times does he (Peter) love him.

Meditation
In this story, Jesus is the all-loving, all-giving provider. Aware that the disciples will be hungry, Jesus, an everyday cook, prepares breakfast for his friends.

The homeliness of this story is very touching and brings to mind meals that I have shared with family and friends. I have memories of the homely scent of baked bread, roasted potatoes and succulent chicken in my mother's kitchen. The kitchen was the hub of my home – where my family and I ate together, shared time together and often solved the problems of the world together.

Jesus foresaw a need in the lives of his disciples – a simple but essential need. We must ask do we see the needs of those around us, and do we respond accordingly? Do we 'turn a blind eye' and ignore others? Let's turn to God and thank him for his goodness to us as the everyday cook.

Prayer
Dear Lord, we ask you to help us be aware of the needs of our brothers and sisters – those who need 'everyday kindness'. Thank you for providing for us this day. Fill our hearts with gratitude for the fulfilment of our everyday needs.

The Wedding Feast at Cana

John 2:1–12

'His mother said to the servants, "Do whatever he tells you." Now standing there were six stone water jars ... Jesus said to them, "Fill the jars with water." ... He said to them, "Now draw some out, and take it to the chief steward." ... When the steward tasted the water that had become wine ... [he] called the bridegroom and said ... "you have kept the good wine until now."'

The Wine

It was customary to serve wine at wedding celebrations in Jesus' time. If the young couple mentioned in this gospel passage had run out of wine, they would have been embarrassed. Mary asks Jesus to come to the assistance of the young couple, whereupon Jesus turns the water into wine. The result is that the best wine is kept until last.

Meditation

This story speaks to us on several different levels. Initially, Mary, Jesus' mother, prompts Jesus to act by saying, 'they have no wine'. How often have we ourselves been prompted to do a good deed by the wise and kind voice of our mothers?

Jesus turns the six jars of water into wine – truly it is miraculous. As the everyday cook, God provides drink for the Wedding Feast so that the guests can enjoy themselves. God often provides opportunities for us to enjoy ourselves in daily life – this may be at weddings, parties or family get-togethers. The use of wine in the story also foreshadows the fact that Jesus will turn the wine into his precious blood at the Last Supper. But perhaps it is the words of the steward that are the most telling. It may be the case that, as far as Jesus is concerned, in our lives the 'best is yet to come'.

Prayer

We thank God for the presence of family and friends and for those extra special 'together' moments. God, help us to recognise that 'the best is yet to come'.

Feeding the Multitude

Luke 9:16

'And taking the five loaves and the two fish, he looked up to heaven, and blessed and broke them, and gave them to the disciples to set before the crowd.'

The Feast(s)

In the Gospels, Jesus performed two separate miracles that are termed 'feeding the multitude'. All four Gospels report the miracle of the 'Feeding of the 5000', to which Luke 9:16 refers. The same miracle can be found in Matthew 14:13–21, Mark 6:31–44 and John 6:1–14. The second miracle, the 'Feeding of the 4000' with seven loaves of bread and fish is reported by Matthew (15:32–39) and Mark (8:1–9) but not by Luke or John.

Meditation

The immensity of these two miraculous stories is striking. Jesus provided enough food for two huge multitudes of people. In Luke 9:16, he multiplies five loaves and two fish. We might be tempted to look at our own 'five loaves and two fish' and wonder what we can make of it for others. Jesus places the emphasis on three things: people's every day needs, what we have to hand, and faith in God.[11]

Let's look at what we have to hand and who we can serve by listening or through the use of our talents. When, in social friendship, we focus on the needs of those around us, especially the poor, and we trust in God, we can accomplish much. The food we eat everyday might not seem like much, but let's remember what Jesus was able to do with the same portions!

Prayer

Dear Lord, we give thanks for the gift of our own 'loaves and fish'. We ask for the grace to help others and to proclaim your presence in the world.

---

11 For further reading, I recommend Charles Pope, 'What Are Your Five Loaves and Two Fishes', Community in Mission (blog), 25 July 2015, http://blog.adw.org/2015/07/what-are-your-five-loaves-and-two-fishes-a-homily-for-the-17th-sunday-of-the-year/.

The Meal with Zacchaeus

Luke 19:1–10

'When Jesus came to the place, he looked up and said to him, "Zacchaeus, hurry and come down; for I must stay at your house today."'

The Meal

The tax collector Zacchaeus was a small man from Jericho, a city that is known as the City of Palms in the Old Testament and constitutes an oasis in the desert. Today, Jericho's outdoor markets are famous for its dates, mangos, lemons and other fruit. This particular gospel story constitutes one of Jesus' beloved meal scenes in the New Testament. Jesus invites himself to the house of Zacchaeus in order to encourage the tax collector to mend his ways.

Meditation

Zacchaeus was a small man, and the gospel story tells us that he had difficulty seeing Jesus because there was a crowd of people present. Zacchaeus climbed a sycamore tree in order to overcome these obstacles. So often, there are obstacles in our own lives that stop us from seeing God, who passes by us each day. These obstacles can take many forms: relationships, work, money. We have to remember that Jesus passes by every day. Are we open to the invitation from a neighbour or friend to eat with them today? Do we make these invitations ourselves?[12]

Jesus has a meal at Zacchaeus' house to encourage the tax collector to mend his ways – do we need to mend ours?

Prayer

Dear Lord, help us to recognise your presence in our daily lives and to overcome those obstacles that prevent us from seeing you.

---

12 For further reading, I recommend Luke Fong, 'Zacchaeus' short story goes a long way. It's our story too.', Reflections and Ruminations (blog), 18 April 2016, https://frlukefong.blogspot.com/2016/04/zacchaeus-short-story-goes-long-way-its.html.

Jesus Eats at the Home of Levi

Luke 5:27–32

'Then Levi gave a great banquet for him in his house; and there was a large crowd of tax collectors and others sitting at the table with them.'

The Meal

In this gospel story, Jesus notices a tax collector at his post and asks him to 'Follow me.' As a result, Levi hosts a meal in honour of Jesus. The fact that Jesus eats with Levi invites criticism from others. Tax collectors were social outcasts because they worked for the occupying power: Rome.

Meditation

Jesus reached out to those who were considered to be on the margins. When he ate with Levi, he was in the company of other tax collectors and sinners. Throughout his ministry, he extended the hand of friendship and welcome, and, as he says at the end of this gospel passage, 'It is not those that are well who need the doctor, but the sick.'

How does Jesus' attitude apply to our own lives? It is easy to extend the hand of welcome and friendship to those we love, but how do we feel about that awkward person we work with? How do we feel about those in our families or among our friends who are difficult to get along with? It is nice to feel that all are welcome at the table of the Lord and in God's house.

Prayer

Dear Lord, we ask for the grace to accept and welcome those who are different from us. Help us to see you in the everyday occurrences of life.

The Anointing of Jesus at Bethany

Luke 7:36–50

'One of the Pharisees asked Jesus to eat with him, and he went into the Pharisee's house and took his place at the table. And a woman in the city, who was a sinner, having learned that he was eating in the Pharisee's house, brought an alabaster jar of ointment. She stood behind him at his feet, weeping, and began to bathe his feet with her tears and to dry them with her hair. Then she continued kissing his feet and anointing them with the ointment.'

The Meal

It is worth noting that the anointing of Jesus takes place at a meal. This excerpt also details the sole moment in Christ's ministry in which he is actually anointed; Jesus was referred to as the Anointed One.[13] Of note is that God chooses a humble woman to enact who Jesus is, thereby reflecting profoundly on God's humility.

Meditation

Here, we witness that Jesus is eating in the company of more distinguished society (he is eating with the Pharisees). However, Jesus reaches out to the woman who is a known sinner. She anoints him with oil, but also with her tears of love and sorrow. He tells her that her sins have been forgiven. Maybe we too have shed tears of sorrow for sin in our lives and have experienced the love and forgiveness of Jesus at confession.

This gospel passage reminds me of a child who has misbehaved at home. She is anxious because she expects to be disciplined by her parents. Instead, they forgive her, and tell her to do better next time. This is what the love of Jesus is like.

Can we use the meals we share with others as opportunities to reach out in forgiveness and understanding? Who are we leaving out at our dinner table?

Prayer

Dear Lord, we ask for forgiveness for the times in our lives when we have failed. We say thank you for your great love for us.

---

13 For further reading on this, I recommend Mark Shea, 'The Anointing at Bethany', *National Catholic Register*, 13 April 2011, https://www.ncregister.com/blog/the-anointing-at-bethany.

Jesus eats at the home of Martha and Mary

Luke 10:38–42

'But the Lord answered her, "Martha, Martha, you are worried and distracted by many things; there is need of only one thing. Mary has chosen the better part, which will not be taken away from her."'

The Meal

In this gospel passage, Jesus visits his friends Martha, Mary and Lazarus (two sisters and their brother) in Bethany, which is not far from the city of Jerusalem. Jesus found comfort and warmth in this home, and he was about to enjoy a meal with them. Martha was active and busy in her preparations for the meal, while Mary was contemplative and prepared to sit at the feet of Jesus and listen to him.

Meditation

In this gospel passage, we witness, once more, the importance of sharing a meal in Jesus' life. He withdraws from the world to enjoy time with his friends. This passage reveals an important point – Martha's life represents the active life of service to others, while Mary's attitude reveals the importance of a life of contemplation.

In today's world, it is easy to become totally absorbed with the busyness of everyday life. There's always something to do! In fact one of the aims of this book has been to rediscover our busy, ordinary lives as sources of spirituality. Let's try to spend a little more time in contemplation. We need to strike a balance between the active and contemplative parts of our lives – between Mary and Martha.

Prayer

Dear Lord, we pray to find you in the everyday hospitality of today. We ask to achieve balance between the necessary busyness of the day and the desire for reflection.

Jesus and the Parable of the Great Dinner

Luke 14:7–24

'He said also to the one who had invited him, "When you give a luncheon or a dinner, do not invite your friends or your brothers or your relatives or rich neighbours, in case they may invite you in return, and you would be repaid. But when you give a banquet, invite the poor, the crippled, the lame, and the blind. And you will be blessed, because they cannot repay you, for you will be repaid at the resurrection of the righteous."'

The Meal

In this gospel passage, the parable of the great dinner is recounted (Luke 14:15–24). In this parable, a great dinner party is thrown, and many people are invited. But, in the end, they don't come! Each makes their own excuse. So, the host invites in the poor, the disabled, those who live on the street to share in his meal. We can understand this to represent the way the powerful have rejected Jesus' invitation to share with him in the kingdom. It is the poor, the disabled, and those who live on the street who will share in the kingdom, not the rich and powerful.

Meditation

There is a beautiful theme of mercy and grace in this passage. Those who are poor are invited. This refers to each of us – we are unworthy to eat at the great dinner, but we have been invited nonetheless.

When life gets hard, let's look at Jesus' example. Maybe those we hoped would come to our own dinner didn't, and those who did were not those we expected. What could God be trying to say to us in this uncomfortable situation? Jesus turns the social order on its head. Let those who come to our dinner table experience his grace and mercy. When we find ourselves at the tables of others, let's appreciate the grace they show us.

Prayer

Dear Lord, we ask you for your grace and mercy in the 'rough-and-tumble' of our lives.

Jesus at the Last Supper

Luke 22:14–23

'Then he took a loaf of bread, and when he had given thanks, he broke it and gave it to them, saying, "This is my body, which is given for you. Do this in remembrance of me." And he did the same with the cup after supper, saying, "This cup that is poured out for you is the new covenant in my blood."'

The Meal

The Last Supper is a festive meal at which Jesus is about to take leave of his friends. The emotional backdrop to this meal is the closeness of his own death, which Jesus feels is now at hand.

Central to this passage is the breaking of bread, the distribution of it to his disciples and the sharing of the cup of wine. This episode constitutes the institution of the Eucharist and is the great prayer of Jesus and of the Church.

Meditation

According to Pope Francis, the story of the Last Supper teaches three essential truths, namely, the importance of love, service and humility.[14] Jesus gives of himself, to eat and drink. We are called to love in this way also, in that we give of ourselves to others.

There is so much meaning contained in Jesus' commitment to share a 'final' meal with his disciples. Love, service and humility inform all Jesus' choices. Jesus knows what will be asked of him. He must have been afraid. Yet, he still puts love, service and humility first. Can we try to do the same? Can we give ourselves to others in our daily lives?

Prayer

Lord, teach us to recognise the chances we have today to love and serve others in the everyday moments of life.

---

14 'Pope Francis: The Last Supper teaches us three foundational truths', *Catholic News Agency* (CNA), 26 April 2018, www.catholicnewsagency.com/news/38284/pope-francis-the-last-supper-teaches-us-three-foundational-truths.

I Am the Bread of Life

John 6:35

'Jesus said to them, "I am the bread of life. Whoever comes to me will never be hungry, and whoever believes in me will never be thirsty."'

The Meal

In this passage, Jesus calls himself the bread of life. This would have had a significance for the people of Jesus' time. God, through Moses, sent down bread (manna) from heaven that fed the Israelites for 40 years while they wandered in the desert.

The name of the birthplace of Jesus, 'Bethlehem', means 'House of Bread'.[15] Throughout the Bible we find indications that one day Jesus will become life-giving bread for the entire world!

Meditation

Bread is absolutely basic to our diet. It is impossible to imagine life without it! It is the stuff of life, because it is so essential to us. I can recall so many beautiful meals that I celebrated with family and friends involving the consumption of bread. I recall being with family in France, where baguettes and wine were as plentiful as at the feeding of the 5000.

The Eucharist has a similar joyous and familial aspect. God has given us freely what we need to live – the bread of life! Let's rejoice!

Prayer

Dear Lord, we give thanks for your presence in the Eucharist, as you seek to nourish our souls.

---

15 'Jesus, the Bread of Life', Catholic Resources, Loyola Press, www.loyolapress.com/catholic-resources/scripture-and-tradition/jesus-and-the-new-testament/who-do-you-say-that-i-a-am-names-for-jesus/jesus-the-bread-of-life.

Finding God in Humanity

The stories of the humanity of Jesus are important because they help us to develop our relationship with Christ. Jesus came into the world as a dependent baby, just as we did. He needed the care of his mother and father as he grew up. We all need this nurturing in our lives. As he grew older, he learned his father's trade – that of a carpenter – and as Joseph was an expert with wood, it is likely that Jesus was also. Jesus is also recorded in the Gospel of Luke as growing in wisdom and stature – something we all wish for ourselves and for our children.

Jesus is the source of love, light and truth. These are important aspects of life. Jesus is the source of love in our lives, but we do not always recognise this. It can be very easy to become entangled in worldly affairs or in the busyness of life. We can be tempted to forget Jesus and his humanity. Jesus took time out to pray in order to discern the will of his Father and to experience a rest from the crowds of people who followed him; we too can rest, regather ourselves and discern what next step is best.

Jesus had a dual nature; he was both human and divine. He experienced temptation in the way that we do, but he did not sin. The Gospels also recount many times when Jesus ate with his friends and with the wider community. It is clear that he really liked people. Jesus truly loved God and he loved his neighbour, and that is what we are all called to do.

The Humanity of Jesus

John 1:14

And the Word became flesh and lived among us, and we have seen his glory, the glory as of a father's only son, full of grace and truth.

In Flesh

In this passage from John, we witness the humanity of God through the humanity of Jesus. The passage says that the word became flesh, which refers to the incarnation, that is, that Jesus was human and lived among us as a man. Jesus assumed a human nature in order to accomplish the salvation of humankind in the world. Jesus became truly man, but he remained truly God. Jesus Christ is truly the Son of God who became a man and our brother, while remaining Lord and God.

Meditation

Jesus' humanity tells us something about God's love for human beings. It also tells us something about our own relationship with others. In the humanity of others we encounter Jesus.

Prayer

Dear Lord, you lived as a man and walked among us. You walked on earth, breathed the air that we breathe and ate with us. We give thanks for your humanity but do not forget that you are divine.

Firstborn

Luke 2:7

And she gave birth to her firstborn son and wrapped him in bands of cloth, and laid him in a manger, because there was no place for them in the inn.

In Birth

Luke's Gospel is warm and human. It concentrates on the mercy and forgiveness of Jesus, his call particularly to the poor and underprivileged, inviting both gentile and Jew to salvation. In this passage, Jesus is born in a manger. He is wrapped in swaddling clothes to keep him warm. We can see Jesus here as vulnerable, both in his dependency on others to care for him and in the rejection he faces because there is no room for him. Jesus shares in the common vulnerability of all human beings at birth. His birth is a humble one.

Meditation

The manger scene is a clear depiction of Jesus' humanity. Jesus is vulnerable and dependent on those around him to protect and care for him. He is rejected, and his birth takes place in a stable.

No one of us is totally independent. We rely on one another every day. Humbled by the circumstances of Jesus' birth, can we try to let go of our obsession with material things and instead focus on care for those who are around us? We need them, and they need us.

Prayer

Dear Jesus, we are very much aware of the love of your parents and God for you when you were an infant and in your life. We pray for children and, indeed, older people, who may feel rejected in life – please bring them into contact with people who will accept them.

Children of God

Galatians 4:4

But when the fullness of time had come, God sent his Son, born of a woman, born under the law, in order to redeem those who were under the law, so that we might receive adoption as children.

In Faith

This passage emphasises and contrasts birth and adoption. The Christians of Galatia thought they needed to follow the Jewish law. St Paul wrote to the Galatians to show them that faith and the cross set aside the law. True sons of God are sons through faith and the promise of God to Abraham, not by actual physical descent from Abraham.

Meditation

Jesus, like us, was born and had a mother. He was also subject to the Jewish law. Through Jesus we all become sons and daughters of God. We can give thanks for Jesus' mother and foster-father – Mary and Joseph – and for our own parents. We can reflect on how Jesus' birth brings us all together, transcending bloodlines.

Does it change how we look on our friends, neighbours, even strangers, knowing that they are sons and daughters of God?

Prayer

We give thanks for the birth of Jesus. Help us to see everyone in our lives as sons and daughters of God.

Wisdom and Years

Luke 2:52

And Jesus increased in wisdom and in years, and in divine and human favour.

In Growth

This passage from Luke describes the growth of the young Jesus. It takes place following the finding of Jesus teaching in the Temple, when he was twelve years old (2:41–51).

Meditation

At a very young age, Jesus recognised that he had been given a call by his heavenly Father. We each have a specific call from God, although we may not recognise it as early as Jesus did.

As we grow up and grow older, we often think about what's next in life, especially when it comes to jobs, marriage and children. Can we take some time in our everyday lives to think about what God is calling us to do?

Prayer

Dear Jesus, you were aware of the importance of God's call in your life. May we discern God's call in our lives. May we be loving people, seeking to grow in wisdom.

Son of Mary, Brother of James

Mark 6:3

Is not this the carpenter, the son of Mary and brother of James and Joses and Judas and Simon, and are not his sisters here with us?' And they took offense at him.

In Rejection

When Jesus visited Nazareth, his hometown, he was faced with rejection. He was known to the people of the area as the son of Mary and Joseph. They did not react well to his teaching in the synagogue.

Meditation

There is so much in this passage that is familiar to us from our everyday lives. We all have been reduced to our careers and family history, and we have all experienced rejection. We don't often think about those who knew Jesus from his childhood, and who may have been surprised or even angered by his ministry. We can identify with the rejection that Jesus must have felt. When we are rejected by those nearest and dearest us to us, we can think of Jesus' reception in Nazareth.

Prayer

Dear Jesus, you were not recognised in your hometown; you were rejected by people who knew you and who would have been expected to accept you. We pray for those times when we, too, feel rejected or unaccepted.

Jacob's Well

John 4:6–7

Jacob's well was there, and Jesus, tired out by his journey, was sitting by the well. It was about noon. A Samaritan woman came to draw water, and Jesus said to her, 'Give me a drink.'

In Thirst

In this passage from John's Gospel, Jesus was on a journey from Judaea to Galilee and had to pass through Samaria. The above passage takes place in the Samaritan town of Sychar. Jesus is tired by the journey and is thirsty. Normally, Jewish people would not interact in this way with Samaritans. Jesus' thirst is a part of his humanity – it is a human need. His thirst opens the way for a conversation that crosses social boundaries and changes the life of the Samaritan woman.

Meditation

We too tire, thirst and need rest. Sometimes we may be frustrated at how quickly or unexpectedly we tire out. Jesus understood the need for rest, water and the support of others. Sometimes support comes from unexpected places as well – like the Samaritan woman.

It's strange to think about, but we can find God in our weakness. In our thirst, tiredness and need God is communicating with us.

Prayer

Dear Jesus, when you spoke to the woman at the well, you were both tired and thirsty. We also experience these feelings. We ask for prayerful help on our journey, particularly when we need rest.

Grief

John 11:35–36
Jesus began to weep.

In Tears

In this passage from John's Gospel, Jesus is crying over the death of his friend, Lazarus. Lazarus was the brother of Martha and Mary of Bethany. It is the grief of Mary (Lazarus' sister) and her companions that initially 'moves' and 'disturbs' him (11:33). Visualising this scene can be a powerful way – in line with the Ignatian tradition – to experience Jesus' vulnerability in this moment.

Meditation

Grief is a part of human life. It's incredible to think that Jesus, the Word made flesh, experienced grief just as we do. Jesus seems vulnerable in this passage, and the image of his crying can 'move' and even 'disturb' us. Our humanity, especially our vulnerability, does not take us away from God. When we are moved to weep, we can think of Jesus sharing this experience with us. When those around us cry, we can see Jesus in them, crying for his friend.

We believe in two aspects of Jesus: his life and his resurrection. He is both human and divine. Even while we grieve, we remember that nothing is impossible if we have faith.

Prayer

Dear Lord, we see your compassion for your friends. Grant us the grace to be compassionate to those in our lives. Let us bring comfort to those who mourn, as Jesus did.

Mercy and Grace

Hebrews 4:15–16

For we do not have a high priest who is unable to sympathise with our weaknesses, but we have one who in every respect has been tested as we are, yet without sin. Let us therefore approach the throne of grace with boldness, so that we may receive mercy and find grace to help in time of need.

In Temptation

The letter to the Hebrews, an anonymous letter, was joined on to the letters of Paul. The letter uses scriptural passages throughout to reveal that the sacrifice and covenant of Christ fulfil God's promises and bring the faithful to perfection. The letter contains a rich theology of the divine and human nature of Christ, together with a description of his effective priesthood. This passage emphasises that Jesus has been tested in the same way we have. He has experienced temptation and weakness.

Meditation

We have no reason to be afraid of sharing our own experience of weakness and temptation with Jesus. Jesus understands these things because he has experienced them. We can be 'bold' in asking him for mercy and grace.

Many of us struggle with shame and self-doubt in our everyday lives. It changes things profoundly to know that Jesus understands. Can we be bold in asking him for mercy and grace in our ordinary lives?

Prayer

Dear Jesus, we recognise that you are a high priest in heaven. However, you were also capable of feeling weakness when you were on earth. We ask for the grace to overcome temptation and for a firm faith.

Part Two
Everyday Images of God

Introduction

The second part of this book draws on five everyday images of God: God the parent, gift-giver, healer, shepherd and teacher. Maybe we have a definite image of God in mind, such as the common one of God as parent – we are particularly reminded of this image when we pray the 'Our Father'. The warmth of the parental bond is often helpful in drawing us closer to God.

There are other images of God that may help to strengthen our faith or offer scriptural insight. It can be so easy to dismiss everyday things as coincidental. We don't realise that there is an eternal presence quietly directing operations on earth. For example, children attend school and often find the classroom a dull and boring place to be – they might prefer to be out and about playing with their friends. A good teacher, however, can often offer guidance in a particular subject that a child may later find inspirational, prompting them to explore life to a greater depth. It is this ordinary presence of the teacher in education that is, in fact, the presence of God at work in humanity.

Other images of God as gift-giver, healer and shepherd are just as important. These images are intended as warm images of God – God has showered us with gifts, looked after us in times of sickness and health, and nurtured and protected us, as a shepherd nurtures and protects his sheep.

I hope that these warm images of God will help bring him closer and aid us in recognising his presence in the everyday.

God the Parent

One very human image of God is as a parent. We can think of the fathers, mothers, grandparents, guardians and many others who have watched out for us. This is the role of God the Father in our lives. He watches over us and seeks the best in life for us.

The traditional prayer of the 'Our Father' underscores our relationship with God as our Father. God is 'our Father', and so we are all brothers and sisters in prayer. The 'Our Father' mirrors the warm relationship that we have with God. The first three of the seven petitions in the prayer address God, while the remaining four petitions address human needs. The prayer allows us to ask God for our daily needs, as well as asking God to shelter and protect us.

In Aramaic, 'Abba' was a word meaning Daddy, and we have received a spirit of adoption that allows us to call God 'Abba'. We are all children of God, but how many of us view our friends and neighbours as sons and daughters of God? Maybe if we were more conscious that God is our Father, we might be more careful as to how we treat our brothers and sisters, neighbours and friends.

The Lord Is Like a Father

Psalm 103:13

As a father has compassion for his children,
    so the Lord has compassion for those who fear him.

The Care

This psalm of David describes God's compassion for all people (103:6–18). That compassion can't be destroyed by sin (11–13) as God is aware of human fragility (14–18). God's compassion for us is like a parent's forgiving love for their children.

Meditation

God is a father to us. We are in the tender care and mercy of God, our Father, who watches over us every day of our lives. God's love is our life, and without it, we die. While many things come and go from our lives, God's love remains. It is with us from the beginning and even beyond death.

Prayer

Dear God, you are our Father in heaven, all-loving and all-protecting. We rely on you for your grace and mercy. We ask you to love, protect and guide us.

The Lord's Prayer

Luke 11:2
He said to them, 'When you pray, say:
Father, hallowed be your name.
Your kingdom come ...

The Care
The Lord's Prayer was the prayer that Jesus taught his disciples when they asked him how to pray. The prayer petitions God, our Father who is in heaven. Two versions of this prayer are recorded in the Gospels – a short form in the Gospel of Luke (cited above) and a longer form within the Sermon on the Mount in the Gospel of Matthew. The Lord's Prayer emphasises the everyday way God is in our lives. We are grateful to him for our daily bread, the daily provision of our needs.

Meditation
We are grateful to God for our daily bread, the provision of our daily needs. In this era of mass production and fast food, we do not lose that gratitude to God, that awareness of our dependency on him. In the modern world, so much emphasis is placed on the autonomy of the individual. We can use the Lord's Prayer to remind ourselves that we do depend on God and on one another. In that way, we can also recognise the need in our lives for mercy and forgiveness.

Prayer
Dear God, our Father, you have given us a heart to love you. Let us know you through our hearts and minds, and let us have the will to serve you.

To See the Father

John 14:9

Jesus said to him, 'Have I been with you all this time, Philip, and you still do not know me? Whoever has seen me has seen the Father. How can you say, "Show us the Father"?

The Care

God is the Father of Jesus, but God is also our Father. Jesus' relationship with his Father and the Holy Spirit constitutes one of the biggest mysteries in the life of Jesus; it is a relationship that is always presented in terms of deep closeness. We know and love God and the Holy Spirit when we know and love Jesus. In Jesus, God has given us a way to know him in a truly world-changing way.

Meditation

Something goes on deep inside us when we pray, as we get to know God. When we pray, we come to know the love of God, that he is near and that he is caring. God is our Father, our carer and our protector, protecting us like a parent does. The divine community is important in our lives, but we are called to live in the human community.

Prayer

Dear God, our Father, you are at the heart of everything we do. We often find the finger of God at work in our daily lives. Dear God, we ask you to be present today in our lives, to unite our hearts with the heart of Jesus and to encourage us to be God's presence in the world.

Father of the Fatherless

Psalm 68:5
Father of orphans and protector of widows
  is God in his holy habitation.

The Care
It is thought that this psalm accompanied the early autumn Feast of Tabernacles (Sukkoth). This included a procession of the tribes. At the time, a foreign power, possibly Egypt, was oppressing Israel. It may be that the psalm was composed from segments of ancient poems. This would explain why the transitions in the psalm are implied rather than explicitly stated.[16] The inclusivity of God's fatherhood is emphasised here – God is a father to all, regardless of their circumstances.

Meditation
God is a father to all, regardless of their circumstances. Can we make our own understanding of family more inclusive? Are we quick to judge people based on their circumstances? Do we fail to show compassion for those who have fallen on hard times, and who maybe do not have access to the support we do? We can remember that God is a father to all, and we must show care for all his children.

Prayer
Dear God, we pray for those who are vulnerable in life, like the orphan and the widow. We pray for those who are in need. We give thanks for the grace and mercy of God, our Father, toward us, his children.

---

16 Adapted from United States Conference of Bishops, Psalm 68 commentary, USCCB (website), https://bible.usccb.org/bible/psalms/68.

I Thank You, Father

Luke 10:21
At that same hour Jesus rejoiced in the Holy Spirit and said, 'I thank you, Father, Lord of heaven and earth, because you have hidden these things from the wise and the intelligent and have revealed them to infants; yes, Father, for such was your gracious will.

The Care
God is both our Father and Lord of earth and heaven. He is the author and creator of all that he has made, including fatherhood and motherhood as we know them. God reveals the mysteries of his kingdom to those who are simple of heart. Someday maybe God will reveal these mysteries to us too.

Meditation
Jesus praises childlike simplicity and humility, as the simple of heart see purely and acknowledge their dependence on God. Humility is the only soil in which God's grace can take root. We pray for the grace to have a humble and child-like heart. We pray also that the mysteries of the kingdom of God will be revealed to us as well.

Prayer
Almighty God, we give thanks for your guiding and watchful presence in our lives. May we, who are your children, always be aware of your importance in our lives.

Blessed Be the God and Father

2 Corinthians 1:3

Blessed be the God and Father of our Lord Jesus Christ, the Father of mercies and the God of all consolation.

The Care

In this letter, this blessing is followed by Paul's assertion that God supports us in every hardship so that we are able to come to the support of others in their trials. God, our merciful Father, consoles us in times of difficulty. His consolation is a form of parental care for us. He helps us to overcome adversity and to come to the aid of others.

Meditation

When we need a kind word of hope and support, God is there for us. He has been present for us in the love and support of family and friends throughout our lives. He consoles us, and his consolation is a form of care that charges us with energy to go out into the world and care for others.

Prayer

We bless you, God our Father, and thank you for the times that you have consoled us. When we experience hardship and suffering, may your words console us.

For God so Loved the World

John 3:16
For God so loved the world that he gave his only Son, so that everyone who believes in him may not perish but may have eternal life.

The Care
God, as father, demonstrated his love for us by giving the best he had to offer – Jesus, his son. He gave us the gift of his son through the incarnation.

Meditation
Dear God, you intervened in human history and gave us your son, Jesus, to show that you love us as a father. God loves the world and each of us. God showed us, through action, that true love doesn't count the cost, it gives liberally. In Jesus, we witness the breadth of God's love – it is not an exclusive love, but a redemptive love that embraces the whole world and yet is personal to each of us.[17]

Prayer
Dear God, we thank you for your love for us as your children. We recognise that your love for us is better than life itself. May your love continue to consume and transform our lives so that you may be our hearts' desire.

17　See Don Schwager, 'The Gospel of John: a commentary & meditation', dailyscripture (website), John 3:16–21, http://dailyscripture.servantsoftheword.org/readings/john316.htm.

This Is My Son, the Beloved

Matthew 3:16–17
And when Jesus had been baptised, just as he came up from the water, suddenly the heavens were opened to him and he saw the Spirit of God descending like a dove and alighting on him. And a voice from heaven said, 'This is my Son, the Beloved, with whom I am well pleased.'

The Care
The above passage refers to the baptism of Jesus. Once again, the image of God as father is revealed to us – he expresses his delight in his son and speaks audibly, so that he can be heard. Jesus is to become the source of the Spirit for all who believe in him. God expresses his care for Jesus in an unmistakable way.

Meditation
God the Father speaks to us about his beloved son, Jesus. But to God, we are also his beloved children, by adoption. Jesus received the gift of the Holy Spirit at his baptism and we, too, received this gift at baptism. God delights in us, just as a parent does in their child. Do we take time to remember that we are God's beloved, that he delights in us?

Prayer
Dear God, you recognised Jesus as your beloved son. Help us to be aware that we are much beloved children in your eyes.

In My Father's House

John 14:12

Very truly, I tell you, the one who believes in me will also do the works that I do and, in fact, will do greater works than these, because I am going to the Father.

The Care

Jesus knew that his disciples would have to deal with trials and adversity after he left them. Jesus assured his disciples that his departure was for their good, so that he could prepare a place for them in the house of God. The same is true of us – when we face difficulties in our lives we can be aware that Jesus has prepared a place for us in our true home, heaven.[18]

Meditation

The words of Jesus in this passage are a gift. Indeed, there is something very homely about Jesus going to prepare accommodation for his disciples, and by extension, for us. He is looking after his guests and his children – he is still looking after us and performing acts of service. With Jesus, we have the deepest personal security in life, knowing that all can be found in him.

Prayer

Dear Jesus, throughout your life, you placed your trust in God, the Father, seeking to do his will on earth. May we, too, be aware of God's will for us in our lives and try to follow it.

---

18   See Don Schwager, 'The Gospel of John: a commentary & meditation', dailyscripture (website), John 14:1–6, http://dailyscripture.servantsoftheword.org/readings/john14v1.htm.

God the Gift-giver

The image of God as gift-giver encompasses the ideas of faith, hope and love. The gift of faith is precious, but, for some reason, it is not given to everybody, nor is it given to everyone to the same degree. Faith in God leads to an ability to trust in him. Sometimes it is not always possible to see the path of life ahead of us, and it is at such times that we need to trust in him.

Hope is not just the desire of fulfilling a dream in the future. The gift of hope is precious. The notion of Catholic hope is that it is 'the theological virtue by which we desire the kingdom of heaven and eternal life as our happiness'. With regard to the gift of charity, it is important that we are charitable and compassionate, as we are called to bring generosity to our relationships with others. And, of course, we cannot forget that the greatest of the gifts is love. It is a wonderful gift to be able to say from the heart that we truly love God and love our neighbour – it may take a lifetime to be able to say this sincerely.

God has given us many other gifts, each to a varying degree. For example, someone may be a great writer or a great musician and bring pleasure to others through their writing or music. Another person may be called to be a great parent – they may have the gift of raising and nurturing children. Some people are given the gift of empathy, whereby they are able to understand and share someone else's feelings and situation. We give glory to God as he is the giver of gifts.

The Gift of Love

1 Corinthians 13:13
And now faith, hope, and love abide, these three; and the greatest of these is love.

The Gift
This quotation is from the first letter of Paul to the Corinthians. This letter was addressed by Paul to the Christian community that he had founded at Corinth, Greece. This first letter was probably written about 53–54 AD at Ephesus, Asia Minor and is valuable for its insights into Paul's thoughts and the problems of the early Church. In chapter thirteen, Paul explains that no gift of God (gift of tongues, faith, understanding of mystery) has meaning unless it is accompanied by love.

Meditation
In the above passage, we see the importance of love. Paul exhorts us to set our minds on the higher gifts. God is love, and God gives us the gift of love also. If we substitute the word 'God' for 'love' in 1 Corinthians 13:4 it gives rise to, 'God is always patient and kind; God is not boastful or conceited.' A worthwhile exercise is to substitute our own names for love in this passage.

Prayer
We give thanks to you God for the gift of love. We ask for the grace to set our minds on the higher gifts. We give thanks to you for your presence as an all-loving God.

The Gift of Faith

John 7:38–39

... and let the one who believes in me drink. As the scripture has said, 'Out of the believer's heart shall flow rivers of living water.' Now he said this about the Spirit, which believers in him were to receive; for as yet there was no Spirit, because Jesus was not yet glorified.

The Gift

In the gospel context, the reference to the living water refers to the gift of the Holy Spirit. This passage highlights that those who had faith in Jesus would receive the gift of the Holy Spirit. This was later to prove true on the occasion of the feast of Pentecost, when the disciples received this gift. In our lives today, we receive the gift of the Holy Spirit during the Sacrament of Confirmation, a gift that is bestowed on us due to our faith in God.

Meditation

We can give thanks for the gift of faith that has been given to us. We can ask for a strong and 'lively' faith in Jesus and in his teachings. We can pray for those who do not, yet, have the gift of faith, as it is not given to all.

Prayer

Dear God, you are the giver of gifts, and we thank you today for the gift of faith in you. Sometimes, it is hard to have faith, to trust in the unseen and stay positive when faced with the unknown. We give thanks for the times when you strengthen our faith in the face of adversity.

The Gift of Hope

Psalm 32:22
Yahweh, let your faithful love rest on us, as our hope has rested in you.

The Gift
The psalms constitute a 'school of prayer', providing us with models to follow, as well as inspiring us to voice our own deepest aspirations and feelings. This psalm is a hymn in which the just are invited to praise God, who is the creator of the three-tiered universe of the heavens, the cosmic waters and the earth. God has chosen us as a special people and our hope rests in him.

Meditation
We all struggle with finding and holding onto hope. Even the strongest Christians can find it a challenge. Does it make it easier to hold onto hope, when we consider that it is a gift from God? Sometimes, we may feel that we don't deserve hope or that we can't find it alone. It is good then to remember that it is a gift that is freely given to us.

Prayer
Dear Jesus, you have 'plans to prosper us and not to harm us, plans to give us hope and a future' (Jeremiah 29:11). We place our hope in you, knowing that you will love us. We hope in you as we look forward to the future with confidence.

The Gift of Charity

Luke 6:38

... give, and it will be given to you. A good measure, pressed down, shaken together, running over, will be put into your lap; for the measure you give will be the measure you get back.

The Gift

God teaches us to be charitable and compassionate; his compassion is all-embracing. The compassion and mercy of God are extended to all, and we are called to follow the example of God and of his Son, Jesus. We are called to bring generosity to our relationships with others. This is a compassion and generosity in love and understanding, in tolerance and acceptance and in forgiveness. It is not just material generosity. The more generous we are with other people, the greater the generosity we will receive in return.

Meditation

There are many ways to be generous. It's not just about material generosity. There are so many opportunities in our ordinary lives to be charitable. Compassion, love, understanding, tolerance, acceptance, forgiveness, these are all ways we can be charitable to others. We can aspire to give and not count the cost.

Prayer

Dear Lord, you are the giver of all gifts, and we ask you to give us the gift of charity. Teach us to be generous with others.

The Gift of Simplicity

2 Corinthians 1:12

Indeed, this is our boast, the testimony of our conscience: we have behaved in the world with frankness and godly sincerity, not by earthly wisdom but by the grace of God – and all the more toward you.

The Gift

Simplicity and sincerity are gifts from God. Paul highlights the importance of behaving with sincerity and directness in the world. It was true in his lifetime, and it is true for us today.

Meditation

Sometimes we are looking for a complicated solution to a problem, when the answer is actually simple. When we think about Christ and his teachings, we should remember the importance of the idea that God is love. Jesus' approach to ethics is remarkably, shockingly simple: we should love God and love our neighbour. It is a simple, uncomplicated teaching.

Prayer

Dear Lord, we give thanks to you for the gift of simplicity. We say thank you for the gift of a simple, unfettered heart, a spirit with 'no guile'. We thank you for the simple hearts of the saints who have gone before us.

God the Healer

This beautiful image of God as healer is prevalent in the New Testament, which attests to the many healing miracles that Jesus performed in his ministry. Jesus was compassionate to those who were in need, particularly the sick. He performed many kinds of healing, working with all kinds of people. We can readily imagine God as an everyday healer or doctor, bringing relief to those who need it.

We give thanks for our doctors, nurses, healthcare assistants, midwives, physiotherapists, occupational therapists, speech and language therapists, dentists, hygienists and all other medical professionals without whom life would be very difficult. We are grateful for the skills they bring to our lives and for the way that they heal us and alleviate our ailments. So often, these medical professionals have placed themselves at the frontline of danger in order to help those who are in need.

When Jesus healed people, he did so in order to demonstrate the love and compassion of God. He helped people physically, but also spiritually, often saying that their sins were forgiven. Jesus showed compassion for those in need, even when tried by adversity, and we ask for the grace to show that same compassion and to trust in the love and mercy of God in times of difficulty.

Healing of Blind Man in Bethsaida

Mark 8:25–26

Then Jesus laid his hands on his eyes again; and he looked intently and his sight was restored, and he saw everything clearly. Then he sent him away to his home, saying, 'Do not even go into the village.'

The Healing

In this passage, some friends led a blind man to Jesus, and the blind man begged Jesus to touch him, in order to receive healing. It is worth noting that without the help of his friends, the blind man would not have been able to find Jesus, who could restore his sight. As the blind man responds to the healing touch of Jesus, his sight is restored in stages.

Meditation

Here we seen an example of Jesus' role as healer – he restores the sight of the blind man at Bethsaida. In this extract, Jesus is performing the everyday role of doctor or physician. Let us give thanks for this gradual and sensitive healing of someone with a disability. The evangelist uses the passage to underscore the blindness that can be found in our own minds and our hardness of heart. These are traits that can hinder the work of God in us.

Prayer

Let us pray for doctors, nurses and healthcare staff who work with the visually impaired. Let us pray also for those times when we have been blind to the needs of others. Dear Lord, enlighten our hearts and our minds.

The Healing of a Leper

Luke 5:12–13

Once, when he was in one of the cities, there was a man covered with leprosy. When he saw Jesus, he bowed with his face to the ground and begged him, 'Lord, if you choose, you can make me clean.' Then Jesus stretched out his hand, touched him, and said, 'I do choose. Be made clean.' Immediately the leprosy left him.

The Healing

At the time of Christ, Jewish law prohibited anyone from approaching or touching a leper, in case ritual defilement would occur. This story is unusual because the leper approached Jesus confidently, with the expectation that Jesus would heal him. Jesus both grants the man his request and shows him the love and compassion of God in his physical touch. Given the limited understanding of disease at the time, this physical contact would have been seen as putting Jesus at real risk of infection. Jesus touched the man and made him clean, both physically and spiritually.[19]

Meditation

Here, goodness flows out of Jesus to cure the leper, who would have been an outcast at the time. Do we treat others as outcasts, instead of bringing the healing power of Jesus to them? Today, the lepers in society are not necessarily sick people: how do we treat outsiders, people of a different socioeconomic class, those who struggle with addiction and immigrants?

Prayer

Dear Lord, we pray for the presence of your healing touch in our lives. We ask for the grace to include all in society, even those who are sometimes regarded as outsiders.

---

19 Adapted from Don Schwager, 'The Gospel of Luke: a commentary & meditation', dailyscripture (website), Luke 5:12–16, http://dailyscripture.servantsoftheword.org/readings/luke512.htm.

Healing of Ten Lepers

Luke 17:17–19
Then Jesus asked, 'Were not ten made clean? But the other nine, where are they? Was none of them found to return and give praise to God except this foreigner?' Then he said to him, 'Get up and go on your way; your faith has made you well.'

The Healing
The above extract is from a longer passage (17:11–19) that details the healing of ten lepers. These ten people approached Jesus because they knew they were in need of physical and spiritual healing. Their approach to Jesus is both a plea for pardon and release from suffering. It is also worth noting that the Jews and Samaritans were openly hostile toward each other – this is why Jesus comments on the fact that a foreigner (a Samaritan) comes back to him to praise God and say thank you.

Meditation
The Samaritan gave praise to God, and he recognised and appreciated the mercy shown to him. His heart was full of gratitude; however, the other nine healed lepers took the healing for granted and did not show their appreciation for God. Are we like the Samaritan or the other nine lepers? Do we take kindness for granted or do we remember to show gratitude to those around us?

Prayer
Dear Lord, we thank you for our lives – may we always have a grateful heart and be thankful for the blessings in our lives.

Healing of the Paralytic at Capernaum

Matthew 9:6–7

But so that you may know that the Son of Man has authority on earth to forgive sins' – he then said to the paralytic – 'Stand up, take your bed and go to your home.' And he stood up and went to his home.

The Healing

This incident took place at Capernaum, where some people brought a paralytic stretched out on a bed to Jesus, who healed the man. The above passage is an extract from a longer section (9:1–8). In this passage, Jesus forgave the man his sins, but the scribes regarded this action as blasphemous as in their eyes, only God had the authority to forgive sins. Jesus proved that his authority came from God because he was able to heal the paralyzed man of his physical ailment.

Meditation

Like the paralyzed man, we too are in need of forgiveness. We long for the acceptance of our limited human natures. Jesus, you suggest that we accept our limitations with gentleness and forgiveness. The paralyzed man was healed both physically and spiritually – we pray for our healing of mind, body and soul.

Prayer

Dear Lord, when you walked upon the earth, you were a great healer. May every area of our lives be touched by your healing power and love, and spiritually – we pray for the healing of our mind, body and soul.

The Healing of a Bleeding Woman

Matthew 9:20–22

Then suddenly a woman who had been suffering from hemorrhages for twelve years came up behind him and touched the fringe of his cloak, for she said to herself, 'If I only touch his cloak, I will be made well.' Jesus turned, and seeing her he said, 'Take heart, daughter; your faith has made you well.' And instantly the woman was made well.

The Healing

The woman in this story is suffering from a physical malady, a bleeding, which has become a permanent part of her life. Maybe her condition is preventing her from being her true self. She sought to touch Jesus discreetly, believing in his power to heal her. We also see how well Jesus relates to people of faith, and it is faith that helps us to establish a strong relationship with Jesus.

Meditation

Are we like the woman in this passage? Do we have a physical or a spiritual condition that prevents our real selves from being revealed or shining through? Maybe now is the time to seek healing and to touch Jesus in a gentle way, believing in his power to cure and heal. Jesus, you give hope when there appears to be no human cause for it.

Prayer

Dear Jesus, you came on earth so that we might have life and have it in abundance. We pray for the gift of your healing in our everyday lives.

Healing of the Daughter of Jairus

Mark 5:41–42

He took her by the hand and said to her, 'Talitha cum,' which means, 'Little girl, get up!' And immediately the girl got up and began to walk about (she was twelve years of age). At this they were overcome with amazement.

The Healing

The above extract is from a longer passage (5:21–43) that provides details about Jairus, the president of the synagogue, whose daughter was ill. In this passage, some people tell Jairus that his daughter is dead, but Jesus intervenes and says not to be afraid but to have faith; Jesus heals the little girl and the people are astonished. The passage shows that Jairus was in a desperate situation and sought the intervention of Jesus, who gave him hope.

Meditation

Dear Jesus, you gave divine hope to the father of someone who was ill. We thank you for your personal concern for our needs and for your willingness to heal and to restore life. You confront our hopelessness and you are compassionate toward the needs of the sick and those with faith. We ask you to be sensitive toward our needs today, especially to those people who are very ill and need your healing touch and care.

Prayer

Dear Lord, you play an important part in our ordinary, everyday lives. Maybe we are suffering because someone has hurt us or perhaps we are finding it difficult to forgive an old personal injury. Dear Jesus, we ask you to intervene in these situations and to heal our everyday hurts.

Healing of Simon's Mother-in-law

Luke 4:38–40

After leaving the synagogue he entered Simon's house. Now Simon's mother-in-law was suffering from a high fever, and they asked him about her. Then he stood over her and rebuked the fever, and it left her. Immediately she got up and began to serve them.

As the sun was setting, all those who had any who were sick with various kinds of diseases brought them to him; and he laid his hands on each of them and cured them.

The Healing

This passage from Luke details the cures of a number of people. It was part of a time in Jesus' life when the crowds were looking for him because they were seeking cures for their ailments. Here, we see that Jesus was reaching out to a woman in need. Upon being healed, her response was to return to her everyday tasks and 'began to serve them'.

Meditation

The woman's response to her healing – the return to everyday tasks – can prompt us to go about our daily life noticing God's work around us and the wonders of his creation. So often, we take take good health for granted. In the future, let's use this gift to serve others. We can remember those who are sick in mind, body or spirit, and pray for their healing and the renewal of their spirit.

Prayer

Dear Lord, we ask for the grace to recognise you in the everyday happenings of our lives. We give thanks for those times in life when we enjoy good health. We pray for those who are suffering with illness and ask for their restoration to well-being.

Healing of the Deaf Mute of Decapolis

Mark 7:34–35

Then looking up to heaven, he sighed and said to him, 'Ephphatha', that is, 'Be opened.' And immediately his ears were opened, his tongue was released, and he spoke plainly.

The Healing

Throughout his life, Jesus was known for his ability to heal. He wished to show the goodness and beauty of God in his action, and he did this by showing consideration. When Jesus was healing the man, he took the deaf mute aside privately in order to protect him from onlookers. Jesus identified with the man's ailment by putting his fingers into his ears and by touching his tongue. With this miracle of healing, Jesus showed his great care for others.

Meditation

Jesus did all things well, and he treats us well also. There is never a problem that is too much for his consideration. He is always on the side of health – an everyday healer. We can trust him to listen to our concerns and to reach out to us with a sensitive, healing touch.

Prayer

Dear Lord, you are present to our bodies in the Holy Spirit, and we affect the lives of others through words, touch and feeling. We thank you, Lord, for the holiness and sacredness of our bodies, and we ask that we care well for them.

The Healing of Malchus, the High Priest's Servant

Matthew 26:51

And one of them [Jesus' followers] struck the high priest's servant and cut off his right ear. But at this Jesus said, 'That is enough.' And touching the man's ear he healed him.

The Healing

This is the last miracle that Jesus performs before the Resurrection. This section is from a longer passage where the apostle Judas betrays Jesus with a kiss. Jesus meets this betrayal with a serene and confident trust in God, showing that his mercy and compassion never failed as he healed Malchus, who had been injured by one of Jesus' followers. These lines from scripture beg the question, how do we respond when adversity strikes, is it with fear or a confident trust in God?

Meditation

Jesus, you faced adversity, and there are times in our lives when we face adversity. Even though Jesus was being betrayed by Judas, Jesus still showed care and compassion for the servant Malchus by reaching out and healing his ear. We can respond to adversity with the same care and compassion for others that Jesus did, trusting in God.

Prayer

We pray for the grace to have compassion for those in need, especially when we face adversity. We ask for the grace to approach God with serenity and trust when times are hard.

God the Shepherd

The image of God as a shepherd is perhaps the most comforting of all. The famous lines from Psalm 23 come to mind, 'The Lord is my shepherd, there is nothing I shall want.' The role of the shepherd is an important one. The shepherd protects and guides the flock.

In today's world, especially in the West, the image of the shepherd is a little more alien. There are still, however, many sheep farmers who continue to shepherd their flocks. The sheep have to be pastured and sheared – they have to be cared for by the farmer. This is true of us too – we are not always aware of the presence of God in our lives, but he is there to care for and look after us. God is our shepherd, and we are his sheep. We learn to trust God and to live in love, knowing that our future is secure in him.

The Lord Is My Shepherd

Psalm 23:1-3
The Lord is my shepherd, I shall not want.
> He makes me lie down in green pastures;
he leads me beside still waters;
> he restores my soul.
He leads me in right paths
> for his name's sake.

The Sheep
Long ago, the writer of the twenty-third psalm heard the cries of those who were suffering and composed this prayer to bring peace and comfort. Experience of suffering is not new to the history of humanity, and the psalmist invites those who suffer to be confident in the Lord who alleviates our distress and suffering.

Meditation
This psalm shows that God is close to us always, guiding us to 'green pastures'. It's striking to think of how often the words of this psalm have been repeated over time and generations – a constant reminder to people through the ages that God cares for us. We can be grateful in our daily lives for the care and attention God gives us to as Lord and shepherd.

Prayer
Dear Lord, you watch over us and guide us as a shepherd guards his flock of sheep. We pray to be holy as you are holy. We give thanks for your guiding hand, and we pray that we, too, may be able to guide others along the right path in the journey of life.

You Are My Sheep

Ezekiel 34:31

You are my sheep, the sheep of my pasture and I am your God, says the Lord God.

The Sheep

This passage and the entire chapter it comes from focus on the notion of God as shepherd and highlight the special relationship between God and his people – namely that God regards, watches over, provides for and takes care of his people as a shepherd cares for his flock. God yields spiritual food to the souls of his people, as he is the tree of life, bearing all the fruits of salvation.

Meditation

Shepherding constituted one of the oldest vocations in Israel, even prior to farming, as the Chosen People had to travel around the countryside. They lived in tents and had to drive their flocks of sheep from one pasture to another. It was not easy to look after the sheep, and it required great skill and courage. The flocks could be as large as ten thousand sheep, and a great deal of care and attention was needed to watch over them. In modern life it can be hard to grasp the amount of work the shepherd undertook.

Can we better appreciate how much care and attention God gives to us in our daily lives? Are we even aware that God's care is there for us, even in the busyness and convenience of the modern world?

Prayer

Dear Lord, you are our God and our shepherd, and we are your sheep. We pray that you will watch over and guide us, tending to us with your tenderness, gentleness and mercy.

There Is No Need to Be Afraid

Luke 12:32

Do not be afraid, little flock, for it is your Father's good pleasure to give you the kingdom.

The Sheep

Jesus tells us not to be anxious about our lives as God knows what we need. Just as God provides for creation, so will he provide for us as his children.

Meditation

Jesus assures us that there is no need to be afraid of the future. Life is a pilgrimage that keeps moving. The kingdom of God on earth could be described as a society of justice and peace. We should try to live a life in love and service in order to build up this kingdom. When we do so, we obtain real wealth, not just for ourselves but also for others. This approach means that we are ready to meet Jesus, our shepherd, at any time.

Assured that God is caring for us and guiding us, can we work with Pope Francis to build a more synodal Church? The Holy Spirit is at work in us too, and we can be an active part of building a better world for all.

Prayer

We pray to live well as your children and ask that you guide us on our journey. We pray for the realisation that you have given us your kingdom and that you will always provide for us – help us not to worry about the future. Let us realise that our future is secure in you.

Like a Shepherd

Isaiah 40:11

He will feed his flock like a shepherd;
>   he will gather the lambs in his arms,
and carry them in his bosom,
>   and gently lead the mother sheep.

The Sheep

God is depicted 'like a shepherd'. Frequently, this image denotes the notion of leadership and of dominion. However, tender and passionate traits are depicted, as the shepherd cares for his flock by bending over the lambs and the ewes with tenderness, as well as by feeding the flock and ensuring that it is not scattered.

Meditation

God is the shepherd who is the companion of his sheep on the journey. God comes with a very special kind of power, subduing all things before him, but much tenderness is expressed in the image of God as shepherd. Can we find ways in our daily life to be open to this tenderness? Are there ways that we isolate ourselves or cut ourselves off from the tenderness of God and of others, because of fear or a sense of unworthiness? God's tenderness and his guidance can both be part of our lives.

Prayer

Dear God, like a shepherd you feed your flock and gather us close to you. May we always be aware of your nearness and of your loving care and protection.

You Are by No Means the Least

Matthew 2:6
And you, Bethlehem, in the land of Judah, are
by no means least among the rulers of Judah;
for from you shall come a ruler who is to shepherd my people Israel.

The Sheep
This passage from Matthew's Gospel actually originates in the Book of Micah
(5:1). It was the chief priests and scribes who quoted this passage to Herod,
who wanted to know where Jesus would be born. Herod was afraid of losing
his kingdom to the Messiah. Here God is recognised in the form of Jesus, as
the person who will shepherd the people of Israel.

Meditation
When Jesus was born, the world did not recognise him as the Messiah, and
it was initially only lowly shepherds who recognised him at his birth. Do we
recognise Jesus in the everyday or do we let opportunities to encounter him
pass us by?

Prayer
Dear Lord, we pray for the grace to recognise you in our everyday lives. We
pray to have a meaningful encounter with you, and we pray that others will
also have the opportunity to encounter you through us. We give thanks for
your role as shepherd in our lives.

I am the Good Shepherd

John 10:11
I am the good shepherd. The good shepherd lays down his life for the sheep.

The Sheep
Jesus identifies himself as the Good Shepherd who will risk his life to save the sheep. Jesus promised three things to his followers: everlasting life, a life that was secure, and that nothing would snatch us from him. We are safe in his hands.

Meditation
Jesus is the Good Shepherd who watches over us. Sometimes, if there is a time of trial in our lives, it can be easy to forget or to to overlook this. We can be attentive to God's presence in everyday life, and we can submit to his will for us. Let's seek humility, trust and purity of heart. Even in times of difficulty, we must be attentive to the voice of Jesus, our shepherd.

Prayer
Dear Lord, you are our shepherd and a fearless leader. You know us and you love us and you value our lives above your own. We give thanks for your secure presence in our lives.

The Sheep Need a Shepherd

Matthew 9:36

When he saw the crowds, he had compassion for them, because they were harassed and helpless, like sheep without a shepherd.

The Sheep

Jesus reminds us to turn to God whenever we face helplessness and harassment. In this passage, we see the compassion of Jesus and how he was able to enter into the lives of others. It is worth noting that sheep without a shepherd can roam in circles and could also be led by a false shepherd. So it is with ourselves. If we do not have a good shepherd, we may be led astray.

Meditation

Jesus is compassionate. He is a shepherd who meets the needs of the people, giving them new hope and faith in the help of God. Can we be compassionate like Jesus, recognising those who are in need? God gives freedom to all who turn to him in trust and hope.

Prayer

Let us pray that many people will find true joy and freedom in Jesus. Fill our hearts with compassion for those who are in need and for those who do not know your love. Help us to bring Jesus' good news to those we meet each day.

The Shepherd Separates

Matthew 25:32
All the nations will be gathered before him, and he will separate people one from another as a shepherd separates the sheep from the goats.

The Sheep
This extract is taken from a longer passage (25:31–46) that deals with the final judgement. Jesus as shepherd will separate people on the Day of Judgement as a shepherd separates sheep from goats. Goats and sheep often grazed together in arid lands as green pasture was scarce. However, at night these two groups of animals were separated from each other because the goats required shelter.

Meditation
If we wish to belong to the sheep, then we must be actively loving people, regardless of the response given to our love. We are called to be filled with compassion for people everywhere, particularly for those who are far from God, for those who may be in need and for those who do not experience the abundance of this world.

Prayer
Dear Lord, grant us the strength to serve those of your children who are materially and spiritually poor. Grant that we may also recognise and serve those who are socially, psychologically and morally in need.

The Chief Shepherd and the Crown

1 Peter 5:4

And when the chief shepherd appears, you will win the crown of glory that never fades away.

The Sheep

Peter gives advice to the elders in the Church to watch over their flocks as a good shepherd would. Earlier in the passage, Peter advises the elders not to 'lord it over those assigned to you, but be examples to the flock'. It is a good piece of advice to those who hold leadership positions in the Church, whether it is a clerical or lay position of leadership.

Meditation

God encourages us to be generous and eager members of the Christian community. We can build up our communities through being ministers of the word, ministers of the Eucharist, music ministers, sacristans, altar servers, linen cleaners, church cleaners, good priests and understanding people who help those in need. Pope Francis has called for a more 'synodal' Church – one that 'travels together'. Are there ways we could be more active in our Christian communities?

Prayer

Dear Lord, we pray for the presence of harmony, cohesion and love in our Christian communities. Grant that we may treat each other with compassion and loving kindness. We pray for wisdom and understanding in dealing with those situations in our communities that are tension filled. We pray for the blessings that are granted to a community of prayer.

God the Teacher

It's easy to imagine God as a teacher. It's an instantly recognisable, everyday image of God. Luke recounts how Jesus taught in the synagogue and was much praised by everyone. Jesus was referred to as 'Rabbi', which is an Aramaic word meaning teacher or master. Jesus taught the twelve apostles, together with his other followers, and his teaching persists to this day, over 2000 years later.

No doubt we remember with happiness certain teachers from our school days. Some people are gifted with the ability to impart their knowledge to others, and we give thanks to God for those teachers who helped us when we were young. It is worth remembering that 'to teach is to touch a life forever'. Jesus too was concerned with the young. He encouraged the little children to approach him, 'suffer little children to come unto me, for theirs is the kingdom of heaven'.

Dear Lord, we ask you to bless those among us who are called to teach. May our teachers find grace, happiness, achievements and blessings in their professional and personal lives.

Jesus as Teacher

Luke 4:15

He began to teach in their synagogues and was praised by everyone.

The Lesson

In this passage from Luke's Gospel, Jesus teaches in the synagogue, and he is much praised by everyone. Jesus was a successful teacher, both in his own time and even today. These days, thousands of missionaries are 'teaching all nations' as Jesus said to do. As Ray Pritchard notes, Jesus never entered a classroom as we know it, and he never received a degree of any kind, but he made the entire globe his classroom.[20]

Meditation

We meditate on the role of Jesus as teacher; he was caring, compassionate and kind. We give thanks for his dedication and his knowledge, which he has passed on to us. Perhaps you can remember a teacher who was dedicated and thoughtful in your life, someone who encouraged you to pursue your studies and your own dreams as a professional.

Prayer

Dear Lord, you are the most important teacher in our lives. We give thanks to you, and we pray for all those who have a teaching vocation or preaching ministry in life.

---

20 Ray Pritchard, 'Why Was Jesus Called 'Teacher'?, Christianity.com (website), https://www.christianity.com/jesus/is-jesus-god/names-of-jesus/why-was-jesus-called-teacher.html.

The Parable of the Sower

Luke 8:4–8

A sower went out to sow his seed. Some fell on the edge of the path ... some seed fell on rock ... some seed fell in the middle of thorns ... and some seed fell into good soil and grew and produced its crop a hundredfold.

The Lesson

This passage from Luke tells us about the parable of the sower (of seed). Parables are important in the Gospels, as they are a part of Jesus' teaching method. Jesus used parables to connect his sometimes complex teachings to everyday life. These parables plant a seed of truth in us that can grow. This parable is actually explained in the gospel itself, at 8:11–15. Only through 'patient endurance' can we hold on to the word.

Meditation

Jesus, you are a good teacher and you have our best interests at heart. You have planted a seed in us through your teaching. We want to have a generous, patient heart that will produce a bountiful harvest. We do not wish to be 'choked by the cares and riches and pleasures of life' (8:14).

Can we try to hold on to the word of God in our everyday lives? Can we be more aware of how the anxieties and pleasures of modern life can make it harder for us to keep a hold of the word?

Prayer

Dear Lord, we ask you to journey with us and to help us produce a fruitful crop.

The Parable of the Lamp

Luke 8:16

No one after lighting a lamp hides it under a jar, or puts it under a bed, but puts it on a lampstand, so that those who enter may see the light.

The Lesson

The above verse is from a larger section (8:4–21) that focuses on how we should hear the word of God and act upon it. Those of us who hear the word must become a light to others. In 8:9–10, we read that even the mysteries of the kingdom that have been made known to the disciples must come to light, as expressed in Luke 8:17. If we respond generously and with perseverance to the word of God, then this leads to a still more perfect response to the word.

Meditation

In the ancient world, lamps served an important function, just as they do today. Lamps allow people to see and work in the dark. The notion of 'light' was also understood by the Jews as an expression of God's inner beauty, truth and goodness. As natural light illuminates the darkness and allows us to see visually, so the light of Christ enables us to see the heavenly reality of the kingdom of God.[21] Do we find ourselves hiding the light of Christ in our everyday lives? Can we find ways to let our faith shine out? Maybe we can show others that light through the way we treat them, following Jesus' example of service.

Prayer

Dear Lord, guide us by the light of your saving truth. Fill our minds with your inner beauty, truth and goodness and enlighten us so that we may clearly understand your way and will for our lives.

---

21 See Don Schwager, 'The Gospel of Luke: a commentary & meditation', dailyscripture (website), Luke 8:16–18, http://dailyscripture.servantsoftheword.org/readings/luke816.htm.

The Parable of the Good Samaritan

Luke 10:36–37

Which of these three, do you think, was a neighbor to the man who fell into the hands of the robbers?' He said, 'The one who showed him mercy.' Jesus said to him, 'Go and do likewise.'

The Lesson

In this passage from Luke's Gospel, Jesus teaches us about the 'law of love'. In this story a man who has been robbed lies injured on the road. A priest and a Levite pass him by, but a Samaritan stops to help him. At the time of Jesus the Samaritans and Jews hated one another, and so the Samaritan makes an unlikely 'neighbour' to the injured man. On some interpretations, the priest and Levite pass by the injured man because of a requirement in Jewish law to avoid defilement. Yet, as J. Duncan M. Derrett has pointed out, the law could be used to justify either avoiding the injured man or helping him.[22] However we want to interpret the actions of the priest and Levite, Jesus teaches us that what matters is showing mercy. Jesus' point, which would have shocked his Jewish audience, was that it was the hated Samaritan, not the educated priest and Levite, who obeyed the Torah.[23]

Meditation

God teaches us about true love for our neighbour. So much can stand in the way of true love and charity. Like the priest and the Levite we often put other things before the 'law of love'. The challenge to be aware of the needs of others and to open our hearts to them is as great as it was in the time of Jesus.

Prayer

Dear Lord, teach us to be aware of you in the presence of others and to be open to their needs.

---

22   J. Duncan M. Derrett, 'Law in the New Testament: Fresh Light on the Parable of the Good Samaritan', *New Testament Studies*, vol. 11, issue 1, October 1964.
23   Greg Forbes, *The God of Old: The Role of the Lukan Parables in the Purpose of Luke's Gospel* (Sheffield Academic Press, 2000), 66.

The Parable of the Master's Return

Luke 12:34–35, 40.

Be dressed for action and have your lamps lit; be like those who are waiting for their master to return from the wedding banquet, so that they may open the door for him as soon as he comes and knocks ... You also must be ready, for the Son of Man is coming at an unexpected hour.

The Lesson

This parable emphasises the virtue of preparedness. Jesus underlines the importance of faithfulness and warns against complacency. Faithfulness is the foundation for any meaningful and lasting relationship. God rewards faithfulness and gives the grace and strength to be faithful.

Meditation

God asks us to be vigilant, so that we recognise him in those we meet. God sometimes challenges us to recognise him in someone who is a stranger, someone who needs an encouraging word or someone who is ill. Our attention is complete when we are fully involved with God.

Prayer

Dear Lord, we pray that when you come, you will find us awake. Please help us to live in a state of alertness and readiness. Please help us to be faithful to your teaching.

The Parable of the Barren Fig Tree

Luke 13:6–9

Then he told this parable: 'A man had a fig tree planted in his vineyard; and he came looking for fruit on it and found none. So he said to the gardener, "See here! For three years I have come looking for fruit on this fig tree, and still I find none. Cut it down! Why should it be wasting the soil?" He replied, "Sir, let it alone for one more year, until I dig around it and put manure on it. If it bears fruit next year, well and good; but if not, you can cut it down."'

The Lesson

What does this passage tell us about the kingdom of God? Fig trees constituted an important and common source of food for the Jews. A decaying fig tree or bad figs were associated with evil deeds and spiritual decline. This parable depicts God's patience, but we must not presume upon it. God allows us to have time, but that time is the present, and we should not waste it.

Meditation

We have time and grace to turn away from worldliness and sin. Jesus reminds us to be ready at all times, however. Our ordinary lives are the place to start! Can we bring God into our everyday lives in prayer? Can we act on the values of the Gospel in our ordinary lives?

Prayer

Dear Lord, we pray to be always ready for your presence and for that time when we will meet you face to face. Let us not delay our prayer life and our good deeds, so that we may receive the grace you give us in your mercy.

The Parable of the Widow's Mite

Luke 21:3–4

He said, 'Truly I tell you, this poor widow has put in more than all of them; for all of them have contributed out of their abundance, but she out of her poverty has put in all she had to live on.'

The Lesson

True love spends lavishly – it does not calculate! This is the point that Jesus taught to his disciples when they were at the Temple and observing people offering their tithes to the treasury. Jesus praised the poor widow, who gave barely a penny because it was everything she had to live on. This was in contrast with the rich, who gave larger amounts of money, but had it to spare. It is important to realise that love is more important than gold.

Meditation

This passage makes us realise that it is not the amount of a gift that counts but, rather, the heart with which it is given. Jesus noted the trust of the poor widow. Can we pay closer attention to the seemingly insignificant, everyday gestures of kindness that come into our lives? Let's try to be generous, and share the many gifts God has given us. God can help us to help others, especially those who cannot help themselves.

Prayer

Dear Lord, teach us how to give and not to count the cost. Teach us the value of true love and generosity, in good times and in bad.

The Parable of the Lost Sheep

Luke 15:4–8

Which one of you, having a hundred sheep and losing one of them, does not leave the ninety-nine in the wilderness and go after the one that is lost until he finds it? ... I tell you, there will be more joy in heaven over one sinner who repents than over ninety-nine righteous persons who need no repentance.

The Lesson

God desires that all will be saved and restored to friendship with him, which is why the entire heavenly community rejoices when one sinner is found and restored to God's friendship.

Meditation

This passage discusses the notion of being lost and found – this is our story too! God is always in search of us, but are we easy to find? Do we hide ourselves from God's presence or do we imagine that we are not lost at all and have no need of him? Imagine what it feels like to be carried on the shoulders of Jesus. Think of the joy, trust and ability to view the world around you in a new way. If you accept the invitation of Jesus to be carried, you will move into a more intimate relationship with him.

Prayer

Dear Lord, we pray for your love and mercy, in order to be reunited with you.

The Parable of the Lost Drachma

Luke 15:9–10

When she has found it, she calls together her friends and neighbors, saying, 'Rejoice with me, for I have found the coin that I had lost.' Just so, I tell you, there is joy in the presence of the angels of God over one sinner who repents.

The Lesson

This parable, also known as the parable of the lost coin, depicts a woman who had lost a coin. The loss was serious as the value of the coin would be equivalent to her husband's daily wage. What would she say to her husband when he returned home, as the couple were poor and would suffer a lot due to the loss. When the woman finds the coin, her grief and anxiety turn to joy.

Meditation

This woman was persistent and searched until she found what she had lost, and subsequently she shared her joy with the entire community. The heart of God is revealed by this passage. He seeks the lost. We too get lost and sometimes forget where our true home is. Can we find time to reflect on the knowledge that God is searching for us? We are precious to him, and he wants us to be near to him, faults and all.

It's so interesting to think that in the familiar story of losing something in the everyday setting of our home, we can be put in touch with the intimate sense that God is searching for us.

Prayer

Dear Lord, help us to recognise those times in life when we have strayed from the path of your goodness. Teach us to remain close to you each day.

The Parable of the Prodigal Son

Luke 15:31–32
Then the father said to him, 'Son, you are always with me, and all that is mine is yours. But we had to celebrate and rejoice, because this brother of yours was dead and has come to life; he was lost and has been found.'

The Lesson
This parable tells the story of a man with two sons, an older dutiful son and a younger extravagant son (the prodigal). The younger son leaves home with his inheritance, spends it extravagantly and decides to return home to work for his father because he ends up with nothing. The father welcomes him home joyfully and celebrates with a feast; the older son is jealous because of the attention the younger brother receives. God is like the father in this parable, he is overwhelmed with joy when one of his children returns to him.

Meditation
In this parable we become aware of the steadfast love of God and the overwhelming joy that he experiences when one of his children returns to him. We can relish in the abiding mercy of God. He is always ready to receive us.

Prayer
Dear Lord, we are aware that you only wish to bless and to restore dignity and love. Please allow us to reflect your love during our everyday lives.